W9-CFO-990

EGYPT

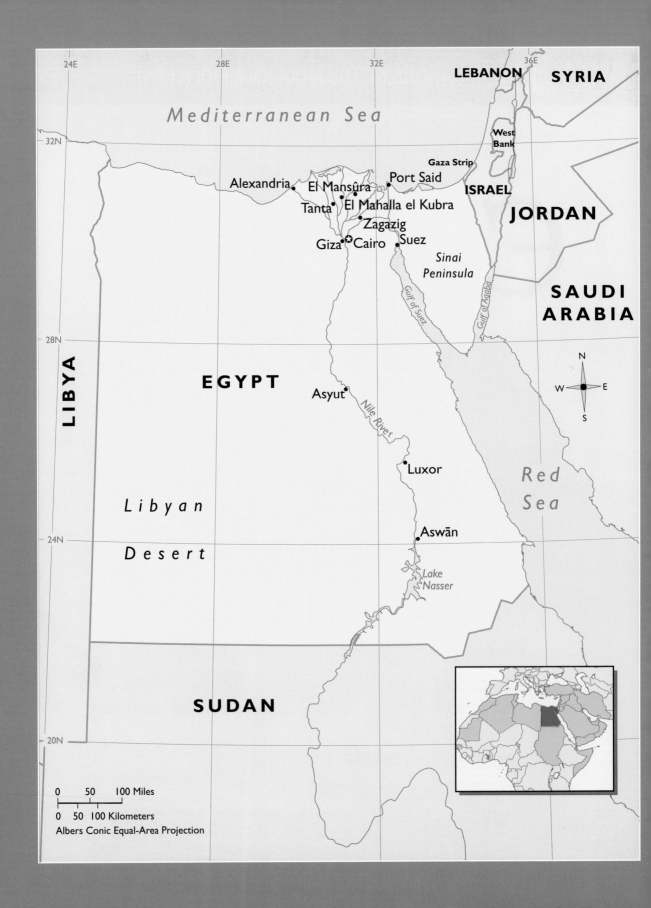

EGYPT

Clarissa Aykroyd

MASON CREST
PHILADELPHIA

Mason Crest
450 Parkway Drive, Suite D
Broomall, PA 19008
www.masoncrest.com

Printed and bound in the United States of America.

CPSIA Compliance Information: Batch #MNMME2016.
For further information, contact Mason Crest at 1-866-MCP-Book.

 3 5 7 9 8 6 4 2

Library of Congress Cataloging-in-Publication Data
        on file at the Library of Congress

        978-1-4222-3440-2 (hc)
        978-1-4222-8433-9 (ebook)

Major Nations of the Modern Middle East series ISBN: 978-1-4222-3438-9

TABLE OF CONTENTS

MAJOR NATIONS OF THE MODERN MIDDLE EAST

Afghanistan	Lebanon
Egypt	Pakistan
Iran	The Palestinians
Iraq	Saudi Arabia
Israel	Syria
Jordan	Turkey
The Kurds	

KEY ICONS TO LOOK FOR:

 Words to Understand: These words with their easy-to-understand definitions will increase the reader's understanding of the text, while building vocabulary skills.

 Sidebars: This boxed material within the main text allows readers to build knowledge, gain insights, explore possibilities, and broaden their perspectives by weaving together additional information to provide realistic and holistic perspectives.

 Research Projects: Readers are pointed toward areas of further inquiry connected to each chapter. Suggestions are provided for projects that encourage deeper research and analysis.

 Text-Dependent Questions: These questions send the reader back to the text for more careful attention to the evidence presented there.

 Series Glossary of Key Terms: This back-of-the book glossary contains terminology used throughout this series. Words found here increase the reader's ability to read and comprehend higher-level books and articles in this field.

Introduction

by Camille Pecastaing, Ph.D.

Oil shocks, wars, terrorism, nuclear proliferation, military and autocratic regimes, ethnic and religious violence, riots and revolutions are the most frequent headlines that draw attention to the Middle East. The region is also identified with Islam, often in unflattering terms. The creed is seen as intolerant and illiberal, oppressive of women and minorities. There are concerns that violence is not only endemic in the region, but also follows migrants overseas. All clichés contain a dose of truth, but that truth needs to be placed in its proper context. The turbulences visited upon the Middle East that grab the headlines are only the symptoms of a deep social phenomenon: the demographic transition. This transition happens once in the life of a society. It is the transition from the agrarian to the industrial age, from rural to urban life, from illiteracy to mass education, all of which supported by massive population growth. It is this transition that fueled the recent development of East Asia, leading to rapid social and economic modernization and to some form of democratization there. It is the same transition that, back in the 19th century, inspired nationalism and socialism in Europe, and that saw the excesses of imperialism, fascism, and Marxist-Leninism. The demographic transition is a period of high risks and great opportunities, and the challenge for the Middle East is to fall on the right side of the sword.

In 1950, the population of the Middle East was about 100 million; it passed 250 million in 1990. Today it exceeds 400 million, to reach about 700 million by 2050. The growth of urbanization is rapid, and concentrated on the coasts and along the few rivers. 1950 Cairo, with an estimated population of 2.5 million, grew into Greater Cairo, a metropolis of about 18 million people. In the same period, Istanbul went from one to 14 million. This expanding populace was bound to test the social system, but regimes were unwilling to take chances with the private sector, reserving for the state a prominent place in the economy. That model failed, population grew faster than the economy, and stress fractures already appeared in the 1970s, with recurrent riots following IMF adjustment programs and the emergence of radical Islamist movements. Against a backdrop of military coups and social unrest, regimes consolidated their rule by subsidizing basic commodities, building up patronage networks (with massive under-employment in a non-productive public sector), and cementing autocratic practices. Decades of continuity in political elites between 1970 and 2010 gave the impression that they had succeeded. The Arab spring shattered that illusion.

The Arab spring exposed a paradox that the Middle East was both one, yet also diverse. Arab unity was apparent in the contagion: societies inspired other societies in a revolutionary wave that engulfed the region yet remained exclusive to it. The rebellious youth was the same; it watched the same footage on al Jazeera and turned to the same online social networks. The claims were the same: less corruption, less police abuse, better standards of living, and off with the tyrants. In some cases, the struggle was one: Syria became a global battlefield, calling young fighters from all around the region to a common cause. But there were differences in the way states fared during the Arab spring. Some escaped unscathed; some got by with a burst of public spending or a sprinkling of democratic reforms, and others yet collapsed into civil wars. The differential resilience of the regimes owes to both the strength and cohesiveness of the repressive apparatus, and the depth of the fiscal cushion they could tap into to buy social peace. Yemen, with a GDP per capita of $4000 and Qatar, at $94,000, are not the same animal. It also became apparent that, despite shared frustrations and a common cause, protesters and insurgents were extremely diverse.

Some embraced free-market capitalism, while others clamored for state welfare to provide immediate improvements to their standards of living. Some thought in terms of country, while other questioned that idea. The day after the Arab spring, everyone looked to democracy for solutions, but few were prepared to invest in the grind of democratic politics. It also quickly became obvious that the competition inherent in democratic life would tear at the social fabric. The few experiments with free elections exposed the formidable polarization between Islamists and non-Islamists. Those modern cleavages paralleled ancient but pregnant divisions. Under the Ottoman Millet system, ethnic and sectarian communities had for centuries coexisted in relative, self-governed segregation. Those communities remained a primary feature of social life, and in a dense, urbanized environment, fractures between Christians and Muslims, Shi'as and Sunnis, Arabs and Berbers, Turks and Kurds were combustible. Autocracy had kept the genie of divisiveness in the bottle. Democracy unleashed it.

This does not mean democracy has to forever elude the region, but that in countries where the state concentrates both political and economic power, elections are a polarizing zero-sum game—even more so when public patronage has to be cut back because of chronic budget deficits. The solution is to bring some distance between the state and the national economy. If all goes well, a growing private sector would absorb the youth, and generate taxes to balance state budgets. For that, the Middle East needs just enough democracy to mitigate endemic corruption, to protect citizens from abuse and extortion, and to allow greater transparency over public finances and over licensing to crony privateers.

Better governance is necessary but no sufficient. The region still needs to figure out a developmental model and find its niche in the global economy. Unfortunately, the timing is not favorable. Mature economies are slow growing, and emerging markets in Asia and Africa are generally more competitive than the Middle East. To succeed, the region has to leverage its assets, starting with its geographic location between Europe, Africa, and Asia. Regional businesses and governments are looking to anchor themselves in south-south relationships. They see the potential clientele of hundreds of millions in Africa and South Asia reaching middle class status, many of whom Muslim. The Middle East can also count on its vast sources of energy, and on the capital accumulated during years of high oil prices. Financial investments in specific sectors, like transport, have already made local companies like Emirates Airlines and DP World global players.

With the exception of Turkey and Israel, the weakness is human capital, which is either unproductive for lack of adequate education, or uncompetitive, because wage expectations in the region are relatively higher than in other emerging economies. The richer Arab countries have worked around the problem by importing low-skilled foreign labor—immigrants who notoriously toil for little pay and even less protection. In parallel, they have made massive investments in higher education, so that the productivity of their native workforce eventually reaches the compensations they expect. For lack of capital, the poorer Arab countries could not follow that route. Faced with low capitalization, sticky wages and high unemployment, they have instead allowed a shadow economy to grow. The arrangement keeps people employed, if at low levels of productivity, and in a manner that brings no tax revenue to the state.

Overall, the commerce of the region with the rest of the world is unhealthy. Oil exporters tend to be one-product economies highly vulnerable to fluctuations in global prices. Labor-rich countries depend too much on remittances from workers in the European Union and the oil-producing countries of the Gulf. Some of the excess labor has found employment in the jihadist sector, a high-risk but up and coming industry which pays decent salaries. For the poorer states of the region, jihadists are the ticket to foreign strategic rent. The Middle East got a taste for it in the early days of the Cold War, when either superpower provided aid to those who declared themselves in their camp. Since then, foreign strategic rent has come in many forms: direct military aid, preferential trade agreements, loan guarantees, financial assistance, or aid programs to cater to refugee populations. Rent never amounts to more than a few percentage points of GDP, but it is often enough to keep entrenched regimes in power. Dysfunction becomes self-perpetuating: pirates and jihadists, famine and refugees, all bear promises of aid to come from concerned distant powers. Reforms lose their urgency.

Turkey and Israel have a head start on the path to modernization and economic maturity, but they are, like the rest of the Middle East, consumed in high stakes politics that hinder their democratic life. Rather than being models that would lift others, they are virtually outliers disconnected from the rest of the region. The clock is ticking for the Middle East. The window of opportunity from the demographic transition will eventually close. Fertility is already dropping, and as the current youth bulge ages it will become a burden on the economy. The outlook for capital is also bleak. Oil is already running out for the smaller producers, all the while global prices are pushed downwards by the exploitation of new sources. The Middle East has a real possibility to break the patterns of the past, but the present is when the transition should occur.

Egypt is best known for its pyramids and the Great Sphinx of Giza, pictured on the opposite page. It was the home of one of the earliest human civilizations. Today, with the largest population of any Arab country, Egypt is one of the most important and influential countries of the Middle East.

Egypt's Place in the World

Egypt is one of the world's most ancient nations. For thousands of years, its culture and history have fascinated and inspired people all over the world. The many names by which Egypt has been known reflect its diverse and shifting identities. Egypt has been referred to as "the Gift of the Nile," the great river that made possible the rise of Egyptian civilization and that has always been at the center of Egyptian life. Ancient Egyptians sometimes called their country "the Black Land," for the dark, rich soil along the Nile's banks, and sometimes "the Red Land," for the vast, inhospitable deserts that cover most of Egypt. In ancient times Egypt was also called "the Two Lands," reflecting the division of Upper (southern) and Lower (northern) Egypt. But the word *Egypt* actually comes from the Greek language—it was a form of an Egyptian term meaning "House of the Essence of Ptah," Ptah being an important god of the early Egyptians. Today, Egyptians generally call their country Misr. This Arabic name may be related to

Mizraim, an ancient name for Egypt that appears in the Bible.

THE ANCIENT AND THE MODERN

Throughout its long history Egypt has felt the influence of other mighty civilizations, including Persia, Greece, Rome, and, more recently, Great Britain. Traces of these empires remain, yet they are overshadowed by the culture that flourished there centuries earlier.

Today, when most people think of Egypt, they imagine themselves sailing down the Nile, gazing at the awe-inspiring temples of Karnak and Luxor, or pondering the mysteries of the pyramids and the Sphinx. However, there is much more to modern Egypt than the monuments of the past.

In some ways, Egypt has changed very little for thousands of years. Most of its people still live along the Nile and in its ***delta***. Agriculture is still one of the most important economic activities. But the government and religion of Egypt have changed completely since the days of the pharaohs. Great cities of the ancient world, such as Cairo and Alexandria, are now modern metropolises with highways and skyscrapers. The ancient Egyptians would hardly recognize the people who work, worship, and play in the streets of these cities.

Today, most of Egypt's inhabitants follow the Muslim faith. Still, the country has a wider variety of religions than some other Arab countries. The Coptic Christian Church started in Egypt nearly 2,000 years ago. Other faiths are represented as well. Most modern

Word to Understand in This Chapter

delta—a triangular area at the mouth of a river, formed by the splitting up of the river into smaller branches as it runs into the sea.

Egyptians can trace their ancestry back to people from the Arabian Peninsula, but some Egyptians have African or European ancestry. All these different people have brought their own customs and traditions into Egypt. The arts and culture of modern Egypt show an interest in the past and a sense of excitement about the future.

Egypt has played a significant part in world history. In the past, it was a major world power. Its location and political significance gave it an important role in the First and Second World Wars. Other, more recent, conflicts involving Egypt may have been regional wars, but they sent shock waves around the globe. The modern nation has many political and economic ties to the Arab world and to the world at large.

So the world has watched closely as Egypt and its neighbors weather the unrest that resulted from the Arab Spring—a collective name for the uprisings and protests for democracy that began in Tunisia in 2010 and spread through the Arab world. Since that time, Egypt has experimented with democracy but this change has not been simple. The country saw an increase in violence and lawlessness, deposed longtime ruler Hosni Mubarak, and then elected another, Mohamed Morsi, who seemed to grab undue powers and was removed in a military coup in 2013. Today, the country faces many unknowns.

 Text-Dependent Questions

1. What were some of the names ancient Egyptians had for their nation?
2. What faith do most Egyptians follow?

 Research Project

Compare the Nile in length and depth to other famous rivers around the world, such as the Amazon, the Ganges, the Mississippi, the Yangtze, and the Rhine.

A Bedouin woman with a camel near their camp in the Eastern Desert. There are about 1.25 million Bedouin living in Egypt, most on the Sinai Peninsula or the northern edge of the Sahara. Most of Egypt's population is clustered around the Nile River.

The Land

Egypt lies at a crossroads. It is primarily situated in the northeastern corner of the African continent, but its easternmost region, the Sinai Peninsula, is part of Asia. To the west and south, Egypt shares borders with the African countries of Libya and Sudan. The Mediterranean Sea washes its northern shore. To the east, the country is bordered by the Gaza Strip, Israel, and the Red Sea. The Sinai Peninsula is also bordered by the Gulf of Suez and the Gulf of Aqaba, which lead into the Red Sea. Egypt's western and southern borders run in straight lines, so that the country is shaped like a rough square. Because of its location, Egypt has much in common with the Middle East but also shares some characteristics of other African countries, and even with the Mediterranean lands.

Egypt's total area is more than 386,000 square miles (1 million square kilometers), about the same size as Texas and New Mexico combined. But only about 14,000 square miles (36,000 sq km) of that area is actually inhabited, as most of the country is composed of desert. Thus, although Egypt is a large nation, many of its 82 million citizens live in densely populated areas.

There are four main geographical areas within Egypt. These are the Nile Valley and its delta, the Western Desert, the Eastern Desert, and the Sinai Peninsula.

THE NILE VALLEY AND DELTA

Egypt's most important and densely populated area is the Nile Valley and its delta. The Nile is the world's longest river, flowing about 4,160 miles (6,695 km) north from equatorial Africa to the Mediterranean Sea. Though only about one-quarter of its length lies within Egypt, the Nile is known mainly as an Egyptian river. In the southern part of the country, the Aswan High Dam blocks the river's flow, creating Lake Nasser, a huge man-made lake. North of the dam, the Nile is lined by modern-day cities, towns, and villages and ancient sites such as the temples at Luxor and Karnak and the fabled Valley of the Kings. After a short but sharp westward bend beginning at the city of Qena, the river resumes its northerly course, gently curving in the shape of a parenthesis. In northern Egypt the river flows past the ancient city of Memphis and the famous pyramids of Giza before reaching the teeming capital of Cairo. Near there it divides into the branches of the delta region, which flow into the Mediterranean Sea.

Words to Understand in This Chapter

irrigate—to supply water to land used for agriculture.
oases—isolated fertile areas surrounding water sources in a desert.
tributaries—small rivers or streams that flow into a larger river.

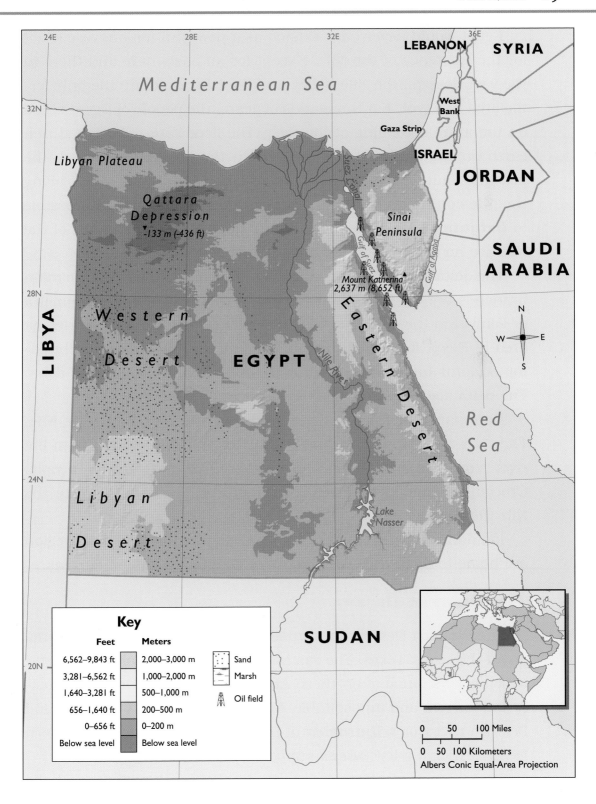

24E   28E   32E   36E

LEBANON   **SYRIA**

Mediterranean Sea

32N

West Bank

Gaza Strip

Libyan Plateau   **ISRAEL**

JORDAN

Qattara Depression
▼ *-133 m (-436 ft)*   *Sinai Peninsula*

SAUDI ARABIA

28N   W e s t e r n   *Mount Katherina* ▲
2,637 m (8,652 ft)

D e s e r t   **EGYPT**   N

W   E

S

Red Sea

24N

Libyan   *Lake Nasser*

D e s e r t

SUDAN

20N

Key

Feet	Meters	
6,562–9,843 ft	2,000–3,000 m	⋮ Sand
3,281–6,562 ft	1,000–2,000 m	Marsh
1,640–3,281 ft	500–1,000 m	🗼 Oil field
656–1,640 ft	200–500 m	
0–656 ft	0–200 m	
Below sea level	Below sea level	

0   50   100 Miles

0   50 100 Kilometers
Albers Conic Equal-Area Projection

LIBYA

Nile River

Suez Canal

Gulf of Suez

Gulf of Aqaba

Eastern Desert

Egypt would never have existed as a powerful nation were it not for the existence of the Nile. Except for an oasis here and there in the vast deserts, the Nile Valley and its delta make up the only fertile area in Egypt. For thousands of years, the people of Egypt relied on the annual flooding of the river. The floodwaters deposited rich earth on the banks of the Nile. When the flooding subsided, the peasants cultivated their land and raised crops. Today, dams along the Nile control its flooding. Although these dams make it possible to **irrigate** larger areas of farmland, the areas on the banks of the Nile are no longer covered with the rich soil every year.

The delta is a flat area crossed by branches of the Nile. The main branches are the Rosetta or Rashid in the west, and the Damietta or Dimyat in the east. The wide, flat plain of the delta is the richest area in Egypt for agriculture. But, as in the Nile Valley, the building of dams has damaged some of the rich land around the delta. The delta also contains salty marshes and lakes.

Date palms and many other kinds of trees grow along the Nile. The river also supports a huge variety of animal life. Fish from the river constitute an important food source for Egypt's people. Crocodiles, hippopotamuses, pelicans, and storks also make the Nile their home.

In addition to the animal and plant life, the Nile and delta region are home to more than 98 percent of Egypt's 82 million citizens.

THE WESTERN DESERT

The Western Desert takes up about two-thirds of Egypt, an area about the size of Texas. The easternmost part of the Sahara Desert—which covers much of northern Africa—the Western Desert is mostly flat, barren, and inhospitable. Much of it is called the Great Sand Sea. No rivers or **tributaries** of the Nile flow through the Western Desert, though a few **oases** support a handful of villages.

There are some low mountains in the southwest area of the

A small Egyptian boat (called a *felucca*) sails down the Nile River. The name of this river comes from the Greek word *neilos*, which means "river valley"; the ancient Egyptians called the river Ar ("black") because of the dark, fertile sediment the river deposited in the region. The Nile, the world's longest river, flows north through Egypt and into the Mediterranean Sea.

Western Desert. In the northwest, the Qattara Depression contains the lowest point in Egypt—about 436 feet (133 meters) below sea level. It also has more water than other parts of the desert, but the water is salty.

THE EASTERN DESERT

About the size of Utah, the Eastern Desert—which lies between the Nile to the west and the Red Sea to the east—is much smaller than the Western Desert. Although also considered part of the Sahara, the Eastern Desert differs in many respects from its western counterpart. For one thing, much of it lies at a higher elevation.

A wadi, or dry riverbed, runs past this Coptic Christian church in the Eastern Desert of Egypt. A heavy rainfall will fill this wadi with water.

Directly to the east of the Nile Valley, it is flat and sandy. However, this area rises gradually until it meets a series of rocky hills and valleys. Further east, the broken land gives way to the higher mountains of the Red Sea Hills.

Unlike the Western Desert, the Eastern Desert has some riverbeds running through it. Although these riverbeds—called wadis—are usually dry, they fill with water after a heavy rainfall. Still, most of the Eastern Desert is even less welcoming to human beings than is the Western Desert. It lacks oases, and the land is hard to cultivate. However, there are some villages along the coast of the Red Sea.

THE SINAI PENINSULA

The Sinai Peninsula is the only part of Egypt not located on the African continent. This small, triangle-shaped piece of land connects Africa to the Middle East. On the western side of the peninsula, the Suez Canal allows ships to pass from the Mediterranean to the Red Sea. Like most of Egypt, the Sinai is largely desert. The southern part of the peninsula is a high, rocky region, with the tallest mountains in Egypt. At 8,652 feet (2,637 meters) Jabal Katrinah, or Mount Catherine, is the highest point in the country. Although the mountains of the southern Sinai are divided from the Red Sea Hills by the Strait of Jubal, they are considered part of the same mountain range. The reddish color of the mountains gives the Red Sea its name. The central Sinai is a high area of limestone. To the north lies a flat, sandy desert.

Like the Western and Eastern Deserts, the Sinai Peninsula is unsuited for agriculture. It does, however, contain deposits of oil,

 Quick Facts: The Geography of Egypt

Location: northeastern Africa and western Asia.
Area: about the size of Texas and New Mexico combined.
     total: 386,660 square miles (1,001,450 sq km).
     land: 384,343 square miles (995,450 sq km).
     water: 2,317 square miles (6,000 sq km).
Borders: Gaza Strip, 7 miles (11 km); Israel, 165 miles (266 km); Libya, 693 miles (1,115 km); Sudan, 791 miles (1,273 km).
Climate: desert; hot, dry summers with moderate winters; low rainfall.
Terrain: desert, except for the Nile Valley and delta; some areas are mountainous.
Elevation extremes:
     lowest point: Qattara Depression—436 feet (133 meters) below sea level.
     highest point: Mount Catherine—8,625 feet (2,629 meters).
Natural hazards: Cyclones, khamsins (dust storms), earthquakes, floods, droughts.

A group of tourists visits the pyramids in a caravan of camels. These creatures were domesticated thousands of years ago by Arab traders, and they soon became a primary source of transport for desert-dwellers. Camels can go five to seven days without food or water and can carry loads of more than 900 pounds (336 kilograms).

natural gas, and metals.

Although the desert regions of Egypt are difficult places for human habitation, some animals are adapted for survival in the harsh conditions. These include gazelles, desert foxes, scorpions, snakes, and birds of prey such as vultures and kites.

CLIMATE

Egypt has a hot, dry climate. As in most desert regions, the heat during the day can be intense—often exceeding 100°F (38°C) during the summer. At night, however, temperatures can be very cool. The temperature varies most during the summer.

Egypt does not really have a spring or fall. Summer lasts from May to October, while winter runs from November to April. Winters, though much milder than summers, are still quite warm.

Egypt's hottest region is the southeast. On the Mediterranean, the climate is a bit cooler because of the winds coming off the water. The coastal regions also receive more rain than other parts of Egypt. In the delta and along the northern coast, a light snowfall is even seen occasionally during the winter. Still, annual precipitation seldom exceeds 8 inches (20 centimeters) on the Mediterranean coast. Although Cairo is humid, it receives very little rain. The Sinai is the rainiest of the desert regions. In general, the farther south one goes in Egypt, the less rainfall there is. Some parts of Egypt hardly ever receive rain. When they do, it is often in the form of a sudden, violent downpour.

The most remarkable aspect of Egypt's climate is the *khamsin*. This hot, dry windstorm blows across northern Egypt from east to west between March and May every year. The winds, which can be as strong as 90 miles (145 km) per hour, cause temperatures to rise dramatically in a short period of time. The blowing sands can ruin crops, cause illnesses, and even damage buildings.

 ## Text-Dependent Questions

1. What are the four main geographic areas of Egypt?
2. How much of the Nile lies within Egypt?
3. Which countries border Egypt?

 ## Research Project

The crocodile is one of the animals that lives along the Nile river. Using the Internet or your school library, research how the role of the crocodile in Egyptian myths. Write a brief paper that explains how crocodiles appear in Egyptian folklore and include a retelling of a story involving a crocodile.

Egyptian hieroglyphs decorate this pillar at the temple of Sobek and Horus, located about 30 miles (48 km) north of Aswan. This unique double temple, built during the Graeco-Roman period of Egyptian history (332 BCE to 395 CE), was dedicated to Sobek, the crocodile god, and Horus, the falcon-headed god.

History

The history of ancient Egypt can be divided into three main periods: the Old Kingdom, the Middle Kingdom, and the New Kingdom. During these periods, Egypt withstood invasions by other peoples, remaining powerful and independent for thousands of years.

In the sixth century BCE, however, the Persians under Cambyses II conquered Egypt, ushering in a long period of rule by various foreign empires. The conquest with the most lasting effects occurred in the seventh century CE, when Arab armies swept through Egypt. Although the French and the British have ruled over it in modern times, Egypt remains indisputably an Arab and a Muslim nation.

EARLY DYNASTIC PERIOD

During prehistoric times, people settled along the fertile banks of the Nile River, growing crops and raising livestock. Over the course of many centuries, the communities of Lower Egypt (the delta region) came to form a small kingdom. Another kingdom grew up in Upper Egypt (the Nile Valley south of 30° N latitude).

Many of the details are unknown or disputed, but sometime around 3100 BCE a leader is believed to have united Lower and Upper Egypt into a single kingdom, establishing his ruling city at Memphis. The name of that king has been variously given as Menes, Narmer, or Aha. At any rate, a **dynasty** ruling a united Egypt emerged, and its kings claimed divine ancestry. This first dynasty was responsible for a significant amount of public building.

After the end of the first line of god-kings, a second dynasty replaced it. The rule of this dynasty, which lasted until around 2700 BCE, seems to have been plagued by regional conflicts, perhaps resulting from competing religious beliefs.

Words to Understand in This Chapter

Crusader—a European Christian knight who was part of the military expeditions that tried to take back the Holy Land from Muslims in the 11th, 12th, and 13th centuries.

dynasty—a succession of rulers who come from the same line of descent (who are related by blood and pass authority from one generation to the next).

fundamentalist—characterized by strict adherence to a rigid set of principles, often religious ideas; or a person who holds such ideas.

Islam—a religion founded by the prophet Muhammad; followers are called Muslims.

khedive—a ruler governing Egypt between 1867 and 1914 on behalf of the Ottoman sultan.

League of Nations—an international organization founded in 1920 to promote the peaceful resolution of conflicts between countries.

martial law—law administered by military forces during a period of war, unrest, or another emergency during which the civilian government may be unable to maintain order.

nationalist—characterized by extreme loyalty to or pride in one's own country or culture, or advocating national independence or a strong national government; or a person or group holding such views.

polytheistic—believing in more than one god.

protectorate—a nation that is governed by another nation.

United Nations—an international organization founded in 1945 whose primary mission is to promote peace and cooperation among the countries of the world.

The great pyramid of Cheops is the largest and oldest of the Old Kingdom pyramids at Giza. It was built around 2589 BCE, using more than 2.3 million blocks of stone, each weighing upwards of 2.5 tons. Little is known of the ruler Cheops (also spelled Khufu), believed to have built this massive pyramid, as his tomb was robbed long ago.

THE OLD KINGDOM

The Old Kingdom, a golden age of monumental building, began with the Third Dynasty and lasted through the Sixth Dynasty—from about 2700 BCE to about 2200 BCE. By this time, Egypt had developed a well-organized government. The king had a chief minister, who supervised the different areas of the government. Outside the capital at Memphis, governors ruled over local areas. Socially, a class system prevailed, with the vast majority of people in Egypt being peasants and workers.

The Old Kingdom is also known as the pyramid age. The rulers of Egypt built the great pyramids that still stand today. The pyramids were tombs, as well as monuments to the power and prestige of the ruler. The Step Pyramid at Saqqarah is probably the oldest. However, the most famous pyramids of the Old Kingdom are those at Giza, near Cairo. The Sphinx, a statue with the body of a lion and the head of a king, is another famous legacy of the Old Kingdom.

The Old Kingdom came to an end during a period of financial problems and agricultural failures. The central government weakened to the point of collapse, and power increasingly came to rest in the hands of the local governors. This time is known as the First Intermediate Period.

THE MIDDLE KINGDOM

Around 2040 BCE, a new dynasty reunited Egypt under a strong central government, ushering in the start of the Middle Kingdom. The kings based themselves at Thebes, near present-day Luxor.

The kings of the Middle Kingdom continued to build pyramids, though they were not as grand as those of the Old Kingdom. Kings such as Amenemhet and Senwosret III expanded Egypt's territory and built fortresses to protect its borders. Toward the end of the Middle Kingdom, many different rulers came to power within a fairly short period of time. Also, the kingship did not pass from father to son—a sign that the central rule was weakening once again.

Around 1640 BCE, the Hyksos came to power. Foreign invaders from Asia and the Middle East, they formed a new dynasty that dominated rival dynasties. This was the start of the Second Intermediate Period.

THE NEW KINGDOM

Descendants of the original Egyptian dynasties continued to rule from Thebes, but they had to pay tribute to the Hyksos. Around 1560 BCE, native kings drove out the Hyksos. Once again united under native rulers, Egypt entered the period of the New Kingdom. It was during this period that the kings began to call themselves pharaohs.

Egypt again expanded its borders during the New Kingdom. Thutmose III pushed Egypt's areas of conquest eastward into the Middle East, and south into the Sudan.

Some of the most fascinating figures in Egypt's history appeared at this time. One of them was Hatshepsut. She was originally Thutmose III's regent, ruling in his behalf. Eventually, she had herself crowned king. Statues of her show a female figure wearing the traditional headdress and ceremonial beard of the pharaohs.

A later pharaoh, Amenhotep IV, tried to change the belief system of the Egyptians. Ancient Egyptians were **polytheistic**—that is, they believed in many gods. The importance attached to a particular god varied somewhat by area and among different pharaohs, but by Amenhotep's time, Amun (or Amon) was recognized as the chief deity. As pharaoh, however, Amenhotep promoted the worship of a single god, the Aten, or sun—and he changed his name to Akhenaten in honor of this god. After his death, though, Tutankhamun restored Amun's status as the chief god among many.

FOREIGN RULE

The New Kingdom came to an end around 1070 BCE. Its last kings were military pharaohs who fought against invaders from Libya and Nubia. Rulers from these lands managed to establish their own dynasties within Egypt. Over the next 500 years, native and foreign dynasties struggled for dominance.

In 525 BCE, the Persian ruler Cambyses II conquered Egypt. In 332 BCE, Alexander the Great defeated the Persians and added Egypt to his expanding Macedonian Empire. Alexander's conquests spread the Greek language and culture widely. The conquest of 332 BCE marked the end of an Egypt ruled over by Egyptians.

After Alexander's death in 323 BCE, one of his generals, Ptolemy, became the ruler of Egypt. He and his descendants—the Ptolemies—ruled Egypt for three centuries and adopted many Egyptian customs and practices. They worshiped Egyptian gods, called themselves pharaohs, and married their close relatives. They also turned the northern city of Alexandria, founded by Alexander the Great, into one of the most important centers of learning in the ancient world. In 30 BCE, following the defeat of the Ptolemaic queen Cleopatra VII, Egypt became a province of Rome.

(Left) By the time of his death Alexander the Great (356–323 BCE) ruled an empire that included much of Asia, the Middle East, and eastern Europe. His conquest of Egypt in 332 BCE was the start of more than 2,200 years of foreign rule over the region. (Opposite) Many ruins testify to the Roman presence in Egypt, which began with the defeat of Cleopatra's army in 30 BCE. One example is this Roman theater in Alexandria (Kom Al-Dikka), which once seated up to 800 spectators for such events as music concerts and wrestling contests.

The Roman Empire's highly organized government and efficient administrative practices, backed by its strong military, enabled Rome to hold on to Egypt for more than four centuries. During that time, Christianity became an important influence in Egypt, despite the emperor Diocletian's attempts to wipe out the new religion around 300 CE.

In 330, the Roman emperor Constantine I made Constantinople, formerly Byzantium, his capital city. This city, now called Istanbul, is located in modern-day Turkey. The consequences of moving the seat of imperial power would be enormous.

In 395, the Roman Empire split into eastern and western halves. Egypt came under the rule of the Eastern Roman Empire, more widely known as the Byzantine Empire. Centered in Constantinople, the Byzantine Empire would survive the fall of the Western Roman Empire in the fifth century. Culturally, the Byzantine Empire bore distinctly Greek influences, and friction emerged between Egypt's Coptic Christians and the Byzantine Church.

THE INFLUENCE OF ISLAM

Shortly after the death of Muhammad, the founder of **Islam**, in 632, his followers swept out of the Arabian Peninsula and began conquering surrounding lands. The Arab Muslim armies scored impressive victories in Syria and Mesopotamia. In 639, the Arab armies turned their attention to Egypt. Over the next few years, they won important battles, finally consolidating their hold on all of Egypt with the capture of Alexandria. The conquest of Egypt by Arab forces was a crucial turning point in the nation's history. Eventually, most Egyptians converted to Islam, though some remained Christians.

The caliphs, or Muslim rulers, appointed governors of Egypt. But rival dynasties of caliphs ruled from different places. The Umayyad and Abbasid dynasties ruled Egypt for about 200 years. In 969, the Fatimid dynasty took over. They were Shiites, a small group outside the main, Sunni branch of the Islamic faith. The Fatimids established Al-Qahirah, or Cairo, as their capital city. They also made Egypt into an important center of Islamic culture and learning. From Egypt, they ruled over a large area of the Middle Eastern world.

During the 1100s, Egypt faced invasions from Syria and elsewhere. The Fatimid dynasty had become very weak and was forced to make alliances with other Muslim dynasties—and even with the Christian **Crusaders** in Jerusalem and other parts of the Middle East. Eventually, the threat of a takeover by the Crusaders led the Fatimids to appeal for help from Syria. Finally, in 1171, the famous Muslim general Saladin ended the rule of the Fatimids and became the ruler of Egypt himself. Saladin founded the Ayyubid dynasty. He also returned Egypt to the Sunni form of Islam.

THE Mamluks AND THE OTTOMAN EMPIRE

In 1250 the Mamluks, Turkish slaves and soldiers, took control of Egypt by killing the heir of the last Ayyubid. The Ayyubids had used the Mamluks in their conquests of new territories, and many of them were generals or held important positions in the government. During the more than 200 years of Mamluk rule, the importance of Cairo in the Muslim world increased steadily. The Mamluks built great mosques, many of which are still standing. They also wrote important historical accounts and attempted religious reforms.

During the period of Mamluk rule in Egypt, the Ottoman Empire was expanding its territories and increasing its power. The Ottomans were Turks who fought against the Byzantine Empire. They built an empire across Turkey and southeastern Europe. In 1453, they overthrew Constantinople and renamed it Istanbul, marking the end of the Byzantine Empire. The Ottoman Empire's area of influence extended as far as the ports that controlled trade in northern Europe. The Ottomans also established their dominance over large areas of the Mediterranean. In 1516 and 1517, the Ottoman ruler Selim I took Syria and then Egypt. However, the Mamluks continued to be powerful and influential in Egypt.

Egypt was an Ottoman province for more than 200 years. During the decades following the conquest of Egypt, the Ottomans expanded south into other parts of Africa. They also used Egypt to increase their influence in the Red Sea area and other parts of the Middle East. During the 1600s, the conflicts between Ottoman and Mamluk rulers in Egypt weakened Egypt's government.

In 1760 Egypt became almost totally independent from the Ottoman Empire. Ali Bey al Kabir, the Mamluk ruler from 1760 to 1766, overthrew the Ottoman governor and brought Egypt's military and government under his full control. He also increased Egypt's trade relations with other countries, especially in Europe. His successors followed similar policies. The Ottomans tried to regain power in Egypt, but they could not.

THE RISE AND FALL OF MUHAMMAD ALI

In 1798, the French army under Napoléon Bonaparte invaded Egypt, in part to disrupt rival Britain's trade routes with India. Napoléon quickly took Alexandria and Cairo, deposed the ruling Mamluks, and formed a French government in Egypt. However, only a month after the initial French landing, the British, under Lord Horatio Nelson, scored a decisive naval victory in the Battle of Aboukir, near Alexandria. Napoléon was in a difficult position. England could be expected to further press his troops. The Mamluks still controlled Egypt's southern regions, and most Egyptians were hostile to the invaders. In 1799, after an attempt to take Syria failed, Napoléon left Egypt, leaving his troops behind. In 1801, British and Ottoman forces attacked from different directions, compelling the French to withdraw from Egypt.

In the years following the departure of the French, the Ottomans regained control over Egypt. The Ottoman general Muhammad Ali forcefully established his rule by defeating the British when they tried to invade. He also killed many Mamluks who threatened his position. But Muhammad Ali was determined to separate from the Ottoman Empire and become independently powerful. He collected large taxes that went toward strengthening the army. At the same time, he forced peasants to join the military and structured his fighting forces along European lines. He created new schools in the Western style of education. He also brought the agricultural system under government management. In this way, he was able to control which crops would be used for export, and what would be done with surpluses. He introduced new systems of irrigation and built a large number of new factories. All of these developments were part of his plan for the modernization of Egypt.

Muhammad Ali fought campaigns in Greece, Syria, and other areas. He managed to expand Egypt's sphere of influence a great deal, but only for a time. In 1840 Britain, France, and other European nations joined with the Ottoman Empire to force Muhammad Ali's army out of Syria. The size of the army was reduced, and Muhammad Ali had to give up many of the areas that he had conquered.

THE ERA OF EUROPEAN INTERVENTION

When Muhammad Ali died in 1849, Egypt was a shadow of the great empire he had envisioned. One of his successors allowed the British to build a railroad between Alexandria and Cairo. The railroad was an important link to India for the English. Another successor, Said Pasha, gave a French company permission to build the Suez Canal. The company built this canal through the western side of the Sinai Peninsula from the Mediterranean Sea to the Gulf of Suez. Ismail Pasha, who followed Said Pasha, expanded Egypt's areas of domination. He also continued the process of modernization started by Muhammad Ali. At the same time, he plunged the country deeper into debt through unwise spending. In 1875, he had to sell off Egypt's shares in the French company responsible for the Suez Canal. Britain bought the largest number of shares. The British became increasingly influential in Egypt.

Because of Egypt's debt, Ismail asked for financial assistance from other countries. When Egypt fell behind in paying off its debt, Britain and France effectively took control of the Egyptian economy. They also gained influence in other areas of the government. This situation prompted members of Egypt's Assembly of Delegates—a largely advisory body with few real powers—to demand that Ismail rein in the Europeans. When Ismail attempted to do this, Great Britain and France convinced the Ottoman **sultan** to dismiss him and appoint his son Tawfiq as **khedive**, the sultan's governor in Egypt. Tawfiq proved to be more easily controlled.

In response to Tawfiq's cooperation with the Europeans, a **nationalist** movement became very influential in the Assembly. In 1881, nationalists in the Assembly joined with nationalists from the Egyptian army to form the National Popular Party. The British grew concerned by outbreaks of violence in Cairo and the growing influence of the nationalists. In July of 1882, British warships bombarded Alexandria. Over the next few months, the British defeated the nationalist forces and took Cairo. Their victory marked the beginning of Britain's occupation of Egypt.

Egypt remained officially a part of the Ottoman Empire, but from 1882 to 1922 it was really under British rule. At first, the British were reluctant to station troops in Egypt. But they soon realized that soldiers were needed to maintain the nominal Ottoman rule and to protect British interests in Egypt, especially the Suez Canal. The British became deeply involved in all of Egypt's affairs. They helped fight rebels in the Sudan. They also reorganized the economy. The first British ruler in Egypt, Lord Cromer, worked hard to reduce the country's debt and to improve agriculture, transportation, and other important areas. Many British politicians took posts in the government.

At the same time, a strong nationalist movement continued to exist. Mustafa Kamil, a brilliant lawyer, journalist, and founder of Egypt's National Party, wrote that "for every living nation there are two great obligations: the obligation towards its religion and its creed, and its obligation towards . . . the land of its fathers." Many Egyptians felt that, with the British in charge, these obligations were not being met. The British were paying very little attention to important issues such as education and the development of industry.

When World War I broke out in 1914, the Ottoman Empire was an ally of Germany, England's enemy. Britain could no longer allow Egypt to remain even nominally a part of the Ottoman Empire. Within a few months of the outbreak of the fighting, Egypt officially became a British **protectorate**. During the war, which lasted until 1918, the British used Egypt as a base for military operations, and Egyptians paid a price. Their country was placed under **martial law**; their economy suffered greatly. None of this endeared the British to the Egyptian people, and the movement for independence gained momentum.

INDEPENDENCE

After the war, a nationalist organization called the Wafd Party organized a group of representatives to travel to London and petition the British government to grant their nation its independence. But British officials in Egypt prevented the Wafd representatives from leaving the country and arrested party leaders. Riots broke out across Egypt, and hundreds of Egyptians and a handful of Europeans died before the British freed the Wafd members and allowed negotiations to proceed.

In 1922 Britain recognized Egypt's independence—though this fell short of full autonomy. The youngest of Ismail Pasha's sons was proclaimed King Fuad I, and members of parliament were also elected. However, the British reserved the right to control their own communications system within the country. They also had control over matters relating to defense, foreign interests, minority groups, and the Sudan. The Wafd was the leading political party, but relations between the Wafd-dominated Parliament and the king were very uneasy. The situation worsened in 1924, when a terrorist group associated with the Wafd assassinated an important British politician in Cairo. In 1930, King Fuad changed the law to give more power to the Egyptian monarch.

When Fuad died in 1936, his son Farouk succeeded him. That same year, Egypt and Britain signed an important agreement allowing the British to maintain a military force in the Suez Canal area but limiting the total number of British troops in Egypt. In 1937 Egypt became a member of the **League of Nations**, with the assistance of Britain. Although Egypt seemed to be moving closer to full independence with the Anglo-Egyptian Treaty of 1936, the nation was still largely controlled by the British.

WORLD WAR II AND ITS AFTERMATH

During World War II (1939–1945), North Africa, including Egypt, became a major battleground. Germany—again fighting against Great Britain and others—seized Libya and moved eastward into Egypt, hoping to take Alexandria, Cairo, and the strategic Suez Canal. Despite widespread dissatisfaction with England's continuing presence in their country, most Egyptians, including the nationalist Wafd Party, sided with the British. In 1942 the British turned back the German advance at the tank battle of El Alamein, near the Qattara Depression in northeast Egypt. Though the country was safe from German occupation, the war caused widespread poverty and hardship in Egypt—which, once again, did not make the British any more popular.

In 1945, shortly before the end of the war, Egypt helped form the Arab League, joining other nations such as Syria, Lebanon, and Iraq. The Arab League's mission was to promote unity among Arab states, to protect their interests and their culture, and to improve their economies.

In 1948, the **United Nations** partitioned Palestine, which had formerly been administered by Great Britain, into Jewish and Arab sectors. This event, which created the State of Israel, would have a profound effect on Egypt. Arab Palestinians objected to an independent Jewish nation on land they considered theirs, and Egypt and other members of the Arab League attacked the new state. Israel defeated the combined forces of Egypt, Lebanon, Syria, Jordan, and Iraq, and by the time a UN-brokered ceasefire took effect in 1949, the new Jewish state had expanded the territory under its control. But Egypt now controlled the Gaza Strip, while Jordan seized the West Bank and part of Jerusalem.

THE REVOLUTION OF GAMAL ABDEL NASSER

Over the next few years, unrest plagued Egypt. Political assassinations and conflicts with the British forces inside its borders led Egypt closer to revolution. In 1952 a revolutionary group within the Egyptian army, called the Free Officers, overthrew King Farouk. The leader of the revolution was Gamal Abdel Nasser, a general who had fought in the first Arab-Israeli war. Nasser wanted a progressive new government, one that would help Egypt become truly independent and self-reliant. The ideas of the Free Officers included liberation from British occupation, social equality, and the foundation of a democracy.

Muhammad Naguib, one of the Free Officers, became the new

King Farouk I of Egypt meets with other Arab rulers at his palace near Cairo in 1946. With him are King Abdullah of Transjordan, Prince Abdul of Iraq, the Lebanese president, the Syrian president, and the son of the king of Yemen.

head of state. However, behind the scenes Nasser was the real leader of Egypt. He headed the nine-member Revolutionary Command Council (RCC). The RCC quickly passed a law limiting the amount of land that any Egyptian was allowed to own. This law meant that a lot of property was taken away from rich landowners and given to peasants and less wealthy people. The RCC dissolved the legislature and made all political parties illegal. In January 1953, the formation of the Egyptian Arab Republic was declared, with Naguib as its president. Nasser became the prime minister.

Nasser established his dominance within a fairly short time. He made important decisions on matters relating to foreign policy and the governing of Egypt. Britain and Egypt agreed that British troops would be removed from the Suez Canal area, allowing for their return if war broke out in the Middle East. Nasser also agreed that the Sudan would gradually become independent. Instead of allying Egypt with the Western powers, he signed an agreement to buy weapons from the Soviet Union. Naguib opposed many of Nasser's positions, but he did not have enough power to stop Nasser. In 1956 Nasser took over the presidency and became the official leader of Egypt.

Nasser, who ruled until his death in 1970 of a heart attack, was a leader of many contradictions. Though devoted to his country and extremely popular in the Arab world, he was intolerant and repressive. Under his rule, there was no real freedom of the press. People who opposed him risked being imprisoned, tortured, or even killed. Nasser claimed to support democracy, but his actions told a different story. At the same time, women's rights improved, the standard of living rose for many people, and Egyptians enjoyed better access to education and medical care.

During Nasser's rule a major international incident occurred: the Suez Crisis of 1956. The United States and Great Britain had previously agreed to help fund the building of the Aswan High Dam along the Nile River in southern Egypt. However, Nasser's pro-Soviet stance strained relations with the Western nations, and the United States and Britain balked at providing money for the dam. Nasser, angered by this decision, resolved to seize the Suez Canal from the British and French companies that owned it. On July 26, the Egyptian leader ordered Egyptian forces to take the canal, which Nasser nationalized. But foreign nations did not stand idly by. In October, Israel attacked the Sinai Peninsula, and the Israelis were soon joined by British and French forces. Egyptian troops and civilians were hit hard, and Egypt lost most of its air force. By December, however, the British and French were forced to depart under American pressure, and Israel withdrew the following March, again at Washington's insistence. The United States, led by President Dwight

Gamal Abdel Nasser, president of Egypt from 1956 until 1970, was popular throughout the Arab world for his support of Arab nationalism and willingness to defy the Western powers.

Eisenhower, had opposed military action against Egypt as a violation of international law. The brief war, though a military defeat for Egypt, actually increased Nasser's popularity in the Arab world.

The Egyptian leader dreamed of uniting the Arab countries, which would increase their power in the world at large. In 1958 Egypt and Syria formed the United Arab Republic, but the union had dissolved by 1961.

In the 1960s, tensions between the Arab nations and Israel increased. Syria supported Palestinian attacks against Israel and, after Israeli retaliation, demanded that Egypt become involved as well. Amid rising tensions in spring 1967, Nasser finally asked the United Nations troops stationed on the border between Egypt and Israel since the Suez Crisis to leave. He also announced that he would close the Gulf of Aqaba to Israeli ships and mobilized Egypt's military. Israel viewed these actions as a declaration of war. On June 5, 1967, the Six-Day War (also called the June 1967 War) began when Israel attacked Egypt, Jordan, and Syria. Israeli forces smashed the Arabs, in Egypt pushing as far as the Suez Canal before the UN demanded an end to the war. In the few days of fighting, Egypt lost thousands of soldiers and most of its military equipment.

Shocked by the defeat, Nasser offered to resign. However, he retained widespread support among the Egyptian people, who insisted that he remain president. When Nasser died three years later, thousands of Egyptians publicly mourned his passing.

SADAT CHARTS A NEW COURSE

Anwar el-Sadat, Nasser's vice president, became Egypt's president. Sadat refused to follow the policies of his predecessor. Fearing domination by the Soviets, he began to weaken Egypt's alliance with the Soviet Union. He also removed many people who had been important in Nasser's government.

In October 1973, Sadat launched a surprise attack on Israel, known as the October War, or Yom Kippur War. Egyptian forces assaulted the Israeli troops stationed in the Sinai Peninsula, and Syria joined with an attack in the Golan Heights, along its border with Israel. Israel fought back, but neither side won a decisive victory before the United States arranged for an end to the fighting. Still, Egypt fared better than it had in the Six-Day War. Sadat had Washington's attention, and shifted into a pro-American, rather than a pro-Soviet, stance. From 1973 to 1975, under U.S. auspices (an initiative later called "shuttle diplomacy"), Egypt negotiated the return of much of the Sinai territory that Israel had occupied since 1967.

Sadat worked to improve Egypt's economy, especially by allowing more foreign investment. This economic policy was called *infitah*, or "open door." Still, many felt that the policy benefited foreign governments and Egypt's upper classes more than the Egyptian people in general.

In some ways, Sadat was more liberal than Nasser. He allowed for freedom of the press and the existence of different political parties. However, he also changed laws to give himself more power. Sadat called himself "Elder of the Egyptian Family." He occupied most of the top positions in the government.

In November 1977, Sadat made one of the boldest moves of his political career when he traveled to Jerusalem to address the Israeli Knesset, or Parliament. The Arab world, including many Egyptians, strongly disapproved of this action. In 1978, however, Sadat followed up his initiative. He met at Camp David, the U.S. presidential retreat, with Israel's prime minister, Menachem Begin. With the assistance of President Jimmy Carter, the two leaders hammered out a peace treaty.

As furious as Arabs were when Sadat had addressed the Knesset, they were even more outraged by the peace treaty. Boutros Boutros-Ghali, who later became the secretary-general of the

United Nations, was Sadat's minister of foreign affairs at the time. Expressing the views of many Arab people, a Syrian representative told Boutros-Ghali: "Neither the noble Arab people nor humanity will excuse what you have done and the reasons of your boss, Sadat." The Arab League expelled Egypt.

In 1978 Sadat and Begin shared the Nobel Peace Prize for negotiating the treaty, which was signed the following year. Despite this international honor, Sadat felt pressure at home. In September 1981, he had about 1,500 of his political opponents arrested. Many of them were members of Islamic **fundamentalist** groups. On October 6, at a military parade in Cairo, fundamentalists shot and killed Sadat. In contrast to the widespread mourning at the death of Nasser, most Egyptians paid little attention to Sadat's death.

EGYPT UNDER MUBARAK

Hosni Mubarak, Sadat's vice president, succeeded the assassinated Egyptian leader. Mubarak continued many of the policies started by Sadat, such as maintaining strong relations with the United States. But Mubarak also stepped back from some of the policies that made many Egyptians dissatisfied with Sadat's rule. During the 1980s, Mubarak continued to sustain peaceful relations with Israel—but it was a "cold peace" rather than a full embrace. At the same time, he worked to rebuild Egypt's shaky relations with other

U.S. Secretary of State Henry Kissinger speaks with Anwar Sadat in Egypt. Kissinger's "shuttle diplomacy" was instrumental in ending the Yom Kippur War. It also marked the resumption of formal diplomatic relations between Egypt and the United States, which had been cut off after the June 1967 War.

countries, especially the Arab nations and the Soviet Union. In 1989 Egypt was readmitted to the Arab League. When Iraq invaded Kuwait in August 1990, Egypt joined the United States and other countries in opposing the invasion. While generally supportive of Israeli-Palestinian negotiations, Mubarak criticized Israel's responses to Palestinian attacks.

Mubarak allowed more freedom in politics and the media—although this fell well short of American standards, and he himself remained beyond criticism. He also worked to make Egypt's economy more stable. Still, Egypt's growing population and obstructive bureaucracy created many economic problems. Islamic terrorist attacks on politicians, tourists, and others shook the country during the 1990s and early 21st century. Some accused Mubarak of using terrorism as an excuse to stifle free speech, but others say he allowed too much Islamic extremism. Mubarak survived two assassination attempts, but his time ruling Egypt came to an end suddenly in 2011.

THE EGYPTIAN REVOLUTION OF 2011

In late 2010 and early 2011, anti-government protests began to occur in a number of Arab countries, beginning with Egypt's North African neighbor Tunisia. The protests—which became known as the "Arab Spring"—were aimed at improving the political circumstances and living conditions of the Arab people. In January 2011, Egyptians began to hold mass demonstrations aimed at removing Mubarak from power. By January 29, it was clear that Mubarak's government had lost control, and the Egyptian army declared it would not intervene to stop the protests.

Mubarak attempted to disarm the protests by first firing his top ministers. He later promised not to run in elections scheduled for September. When these steps did not appease the protesters, he resigned as president on February 11, 2011, and fled the country.

Thousands of Egyptians gathered in Cairo's Tahrir Square to demand political reforms in January 2011. The protests, which soon spread throughout Egypt, forced longtime leader Hosni Mubarak to resign from office and leave the country.

Commanders of the Egyptian military soon announced that the constitution and the parliament of Egypt had been dissolved, and that new elections would be held later in the year. The protests continued throughout 2011, as many people were worried that the military would attempt to maintain control over the government indefinitely.

 ## Text-Dependent Questions

1. What group conquered Egypt in the sixth century?
2. Which kingdom is known as the pyramid age?
3. Who made Egypt an important center of Islamic culture?

 ## Research Project

When the Roman Empire split, Egypt became part of the Eastern Roman Empire, also known as the Byzantine Empire. The adjective "byzantine" can be used to describe something that is intricate, complex, and in some cases dishonest. Use the Internet or your school library to research the history of the Byzantine Empire and write two to three paragraphs explaining why you think the adjective *byzantine* does or does not accurately describe the Eastern Roman Empire.

In June 2013, two years after the Egyptian revolution that overthrew the Mubarak regime, millions of people took to the streets again to protest the policies of Mohamed Morsi, who had been elected president in 2012. This photo shows a public square in Alexandria. In July 2013, the military deposed Morsi and established a new government.

Politics, the Economy, and Religion

Throughout its history, Egypt has seen many political systems come and go. Pharaohs, sultans, kings, presidents, and representatives of other nations have all governed the country in different ways. Since 2011, the political system has been completely overturned.

When Egypt won independence from Great Britain in 1922, its government became a constitutional monarchy. Officially, the king was the ruler of the country, and he could make certain decisions about the running of Parliament and the selection of government officials, but the constitution limited his power. Egyptian men, but not women, received the right to vote in general elections. The political party that won these elections became the dominant party in Parliament. For many years, this was the nationalist Wafd Party. During Egypt's years as a constitutional monarchy, there was a constant power struggle between the king, the Wafd, and the British. The British supported or opposed the king and the Wafd as

49

it suited their needs. In the 1930s, extreme political groups such as the Muslim Brotherhood and Young Egypt became more influential. Other political groups broke off from the Wafd.

THE EGYPTIAN REPUBLIC

Egypt became a ***republic*** in 1953, ending the rule of the monarchy. At that time, all political parties were made illegal. A new constitution came into effect, and the president became more powerful than the Parliament.

In 1962 Nasser's government laid down a charter of rules for the governing of the country. The charter included the formation of the only legal political party, the Arab Socialist Union (ASU). All Egyptians were to support the ASU. In the next few years, the National Assembly came into being. It was a form of Parliament where all the representatives were members of the ASU. All areas of the country were represented. Half of the seats were reserved for workers or farmers. Several women also became representatives in the National Assembly. The president himself appointed 10 representatives. The power of the president over the Assembly included the right to dissolve it. Although the government was supposed to

Words to Understand in This Chapter

fasting—voluntarily going without food for a period of time, often for religious reasons.
gross domestic product (GDP)—the total value of goods and services a nation produces in a one-year period.
inflation—rising prices of goods, usually because of an increase in the supply of money from the government.
judicial—related to judges or courts of law.
monotheism—the belief that there is only one God.
orthodox—generally accepted or approved, especially in religion.
republic—a nation in which power resides in the hands of citizens entitled to vote and is exercised by their elected representatives acting in their behalf.
textiles—fabrics or cloth.

Egypt's red, white, and black flag design includes a yellow Eagle of Saladin (a popular symbol of the 12th-century Muslim leader). The Arabic writing on the crest in the eagle's talons reads, "The Arab Republic of Egypt." This version of the flag was adopted on October 4, 1984.

be democratic, it was more of a dictatorship.

In the 1970s Sadat tried to be more democratic than Nasser had been. The legislature, renamed the People's Assembly in the new constitution of 1971, was more powerful than it had been in the past. Political parties were legalized once again. Officially, political parties based on religion were still prohibited. But Sadat permitted the existence of the Muslim Brotherhood—an Islamic fundamentalist organization established in the late 1920s. Though its members could not run for office under the banner of the Muslim Brotherhood, some won election as independents or as candidates from other parties. (Sadat would eventually crack down on the Muslim Brotherhood, which vocally opposed peace with Israel, and some of its members were involved in his assassination.)

In some ways Mubarak's government allowed a greater degree of political freedom. During his rule more political parties existed than under Nasser or Sadat. The media was also permitted to express its views more openly. But the government also controls the limits of political expression and the government-sponsored political party dominated the legislature. Mubarak also continued to enforce laws designed to stop terrorist groups, as the country was officially oper-

Hosni Mubarak (right) meets with U.N. Secretary-General Ban Ki-moon in Cairo, 2009. Mubarak ruled Egypt from 1981 until 2012, when he was forced to resign. Mubarak was later arrested and sentenced to prison on corruption chargers; although the conviction was overturned, he remained in an Egyptian prison.

ating under a "state of emergency" from 1981 until 2012. Attacks on foreign tourists since the 1990s led to a vigorous repression of terrorism.

Unfortunately, observers both inside Egypt and abroad agreed that during the Mubarak regime, elections were anything but fair. In the fall of 2010, amid allegations of ballot stuffing and voter intimidation, the NDP's two biggest opposition parties—the Muslim Brotherhood and the Waft party—both boycotted the run-off voting for seats in the People's Assembly. As a result, the NDP won approximately 97 percent of the seats by default.

Thanks to the unrest that followed the Arab Spring, the Muslim Brotherhood had an opportunity to come into power. When Mubarak resigned, Egypt's military governed the country for six months, until elections could be held. In June 2012, Muslim Brotherhood candidate Mohamed Morsi was elected president. He defeated Ahmed Shafik, a former official from Mubarak's government.

The Muslim Brotherhood and the military soon clashed over control of the country. Morsi oversaw the drafting of a new constitution in 2012. However, he was criticized for trying to extend his powers as president, and some Egyptians became disillusioned since his government did not seem to be as democratic as they had hoped. By June 2013, many Egyptians were demonstrating in the streets again, this time calling for Morsi to be removed from office. The military removed Morsi the following month in a coup d'état led by General Abdel Fattah el-Sisi. Adly Mansour, a judge, became Egypt's interim president, but it was clear that Sisi and the military were running the country. Morsi's supporters protested his removal, but the military cracked down on dissent. Eventually, the military-backed interim government banned the Muslim Brotherhood.

Mohamed Morsi angered many Egyptians when he declared that his decisions would not be subject to judicial oversight. After his ouster Morsi was arrested, and in the spring of 2015 he was sentenced to 20 years in prison for inciting violence during his term in office.

In May 2014, Egyptians voted for a new constitution and elected el-Sisi to be their president. Elections for a new parliament were scheduled for 2015, although they have been delayed several times.

The 2014 constitution is similar to Egypt's 1971 constitution, which was in force until the 2011 revolution. The new constitution is based both on Western forms of law and on Islamic law. The Egyptian president can appoint and dismiss government ministers, including the prime minister. However, the military retains the right to appoint the minister of defense until 2022. The president commands the armed forces and has near complete control over the government as a whole. The president is elected for a four-year term, and can serve two terms.

Below the level of national government, there are 26 political areas called governorates in Egypt. Each has a governor. The governorates are divided into the smaller areas of districts, counties,

General Abdel Fattah el-Sisi led the 2013 coup that removed Morsi from the presidency. He was elected president of Egypt in 2014.

and villages. Egypt's largest cities, including Cairo and Alexandria, are considered governorates. The elected council members at each level of local government make decisions for their areas about health, education, housing, and other matters.

The Egyptian *judicial* system is based on Islamic, British, French, and Italian law. It has several levels of courts. At the highest level is the Supreme Court, which interprets laws and can make a final decision when lower courts disagree on the same matter. Although the president appoints Supreme Court judges, these judges do not have to answer to him. The Court of Cassation is the highest court that normally deals with criminal cases. There are no jury trials in the Egyptian courts; judges decide a defendant's guilt or innocence. Below the Court of Cassation, district and regional courts deal with minor cases. Courts of appeal hear appeals of decisions made by the lower courts.

ECONOMIC OVERVIEW

Egypt has great economic potential. It contains a wide variety of natural resources, including petroleum, natural gas, iron ore, and uranium. In addition, its fabulous historical treasures make Egypt an attractive tourist destination. Nevertheless, the nation faces some difficult economic challenges, including a huge foreign debt and problems stemming from its rapidly growing population.

For thousands of years, most Egyptians worked in agriculture. Egypt produced food and clothing for its own people and exported crops to other nations. During the 19th century, rulers such as

Muhammad Ali were eager to modernize Egypt. Other nations with interests in Egypt saw its potential for economic growth as well. Cotton production became Egypt's primary economic activity.

During the 1930s and World War II, Egypt began to develop other industries. Factories were constructed, and the nation began producing goods and services besides cotton on a large scale.

In the 1950s and 1960s, Nasser brought most of Egypt's major economic activity under government control. His goals were to counteract the growing gap between the rich and the poor, and to limit the amount of property that individuals could own. The government appointed people to run major companies. It also decided what kinds of goods the country should produce and established the prices for those goods. Too much government control produced **inflation**, problems with fixed pricing despite rising costs, and a stagnant economy.

In the 1970s Sadat's *infitah*, or open-door policy, allowed for much more foreign investment in Egypt. Egypt also accepted more financial aid from other countries, especially the United States. These policies helped boost the economy. However, they also caused higher inflation rates and more extremes of wealth and poverty. Projects such as the Aswan High Dam have had positive and negative effects. The Aswan High Dam is an important power source. It allows much more land to be used for agriculture than was possible before. However, many Egyptians were displaced by the building of the dam. The dam has also lowered the quality of the soil on the banks of the Nile.

Egypt is currently in the process of returning to an economy with less government involvement and more private ownership. The pace of this privatization effort, however, has been quite slow. Still, foreign investors believe that Egypt has great possibilities for economic growth. Overall, though, Egypt's economy remains weak. The economy cannot keep up with the nation's rapid population

(Left) The Khan el-Khalili bazaar in Cairo is a busy shopping district. (Opposite) A farmer works in his field in the Nile Valley. Agriculture employs about one-third of Egypt's people.

growth. Egypt has to import more goods than it exports, increasing the weight of foreign debt. The unemployment rate is chronically high. The cost of living is low, but so are the wages earned by most workers. Workers in the mining and manufacturing industries earn higher wages, while the lowest wages go to people working in agriculture, outside of the cities.

According to statistics compiled by the World Bank, Egypt's **gross domestic product (GDP)** in 2014 stood at $945.4 billion billion. (GDP—the total value of the goods and services a country produces in a one-year period—is an important measure of an economy's overall size.) In 2014, Egypt had the world's 24th-largest economy, roughly equal to Poland or Argentina. By Western standards Egypt is a poor country, though it is considered a middle-income nation when compared with the entire world.

ECONOMIC SECTORS

Agriculture, once the foundation of Egyptian society, today accounts for less than 20 percent of Egypt's GDP. Although Egypt produces millions of tons of food crops, the country must also import food to feed its growing population. Still, about a third of the Egyptian labor force works in farming, which by Western standards is quite high. Some aspects of agriculture are mechanized, but others continue to be done much as they were thousands of years ago. Many farmers still use cattle to drag their plows across the fields. In the past, farmers could only plant crops after the flooding of the Nile, which deposited a layer of rich soil and watered their fields. Because of the building of the Aswan High Dam and other changes in the irrigation systems, crops can be planted at any time of the year. Cotton, rice, wheat, sugarcane, and tomatoes are some of the most important crops. More than one-fifth of the available agricultural land at any time is used for cotton, since it is such an important export. But the government insists that farmers use a certain amount of land for food production. Farmers also raise livestock such as cattle, sheep, goats, and chickens. Fish, a major Egyptian food source, come from the Nile, the Mediterranean, the Red Sea, and fisheries on Lake Nasser.

Industry is responsible for about two-fifths of Egypt's GDP.

Egyptian industry includes mining, manufacturing, and construction. Most of the country's mines are located near the Red Sea or on the Sinai Peninsula. Most of its oil production is centered in those areas as well. Egypt both uses and exports a great deal of natural gas. Other important mining industries include iron and salt. **Textiles**, especially cotton textiles, are Egypt's most important manufacturing industry. Egypt also has factories for rubber, processed foods, and furniture, among others. Cities based around factories have sprung up near Cairo and in other areas.

Services account for about half of Egypt's GDP. A significant proportion of this total comes from government-provided services, including health care and education. Other important contributors to the service sector include stores, banks, real estate, and transportation.

TOURISM

Tourism has become a crucial part of Egypt's economy. More than 10 percent of Egypt's people may be involved in the tourist industry in some capacity—many working part-time to supplement their income from other jobs. Millions of tourists from all over the world visit Egypt every year. For many people, Egypt is appealing not only because it boasts natural beauty and an unparalleled history, but also because it is a relatively inexpensive place to visit. Popular tours include a visit to Cairo and the pyramids at Giza, followed by a trip down the Nile to Luxor. Other tourists visit resorts on the Mediterranean and the Red Sea. The Nile offers floating hotels and luxury cruises.

Over the years, the number of tourists traveling to Egypt has fluctuated with political developments. For decades, many tourists came from other Arab countries, but Sadat's peace treaty with Israel in the late 1970s made Egypt unpopular with Arab visitors. Tourism also suffered in the 1990s, with increased activity by terrorist groups. A deadly attack on tourists at Luxor in 1997 sent the industry into an immediate slump, but Egypt worked hard to reestablish itself as a popular destination and by 2002 record numbers of foreigners were visiting Egypt's historic sites and Red Sea resorts. However, another outbreak of terrorist attacks occurred in 2005, when the resort towns of Sharm al-Sheikh, Taba, and Ras Shitan were rocked by bombings; in April 2006 at the Red Sea resort of Dahab; and in 2009, when tourists were targeted in Cairo.

The instability that followed the 2011 revolution crippled Egypt's tourism industry, and entire towns that were dependent on the money that visitors spend were affected. Conflicts elsewhere in the Middle East, such as Syria and Iraq, have also reduced the number of foreign visitors to Egypt.

RELIGION

According to the 2014 constitution, the official religion of Egypt is Islam, a **monotheistic** faith.

Islam was founded around the year 610 CE, when the prophet Muhammad, an Arab merchant living in Mecca, claimed to have been visited by an angel of Allah (God). Muhammad began to preach God's revealed message, first secretly to family members, friends, and a few others, then publicly. The core of his message—that there is only one true God—did not sit well among the idol-worshipping, polytheistic Meccans. Eventually, in 622, persecution forced Muhammad and his followers—called Muslims—to flee to the oasis town of Medina. That event, known as the Hegira, or *Hijrah*, marks the beginning of the Islamic era. After several years of warfare, Muhammad and his followers took Mecca, in 629. By the time of his death in 632, the entire Arabian Peninsula had come under the influence of Islam. In the following decades, Muslims would spread their religion—and build a large empire—through conquest.

Muslims believe that there is only one God, that Muhammad is his

The Sultan Hassan Mosque, located in Cairo, was built in 1256.

last and most important prophet, and that God's words are contained in the Qur'an (also spelled "Koran"), a collection of revelations received by Muhammad. But they also believe that the Bible is a holy book and that Abraham, Moses, Jesus, and other figures from the **Judeo-Christian** tradition were prophets as well.

About 90 percent of all Egyptians practice the Muslim faith. Almost all of them belong to the Sunni branch of Islam, which is viewed as the **orthodox** branch. A very small number belong to the Shiite branch. The Sunnis and the Shiites separated from each other not long after the foundation of Islam.

Sunni Muslims believe that the first four caliphs after the death of Muhammad were the rightful leaders of Islam. They accept that caliphs can be appointed, and that they do not have to be related to Muhammad. Sunni Muslims also believe strongly in the importance of tradition. In addition to the Holy Qur'an, they accept the

Hadith, a collection of sayings traditionally attributed to Muhammad.

Shiite Muslims believe that only a descendant of Muhammad has the right to be a caliph. In their view Ali, Muhammad's cousin and son-in-law, was the first legitimate caliph, though he was historically Islam's fourth caliph after Muhammad. When Ali was assassinated in 661, the Shiites broke off from the rest of Islam. Today they constitute a minority of Muslims worldwide, though in a few parts of the Arab world they are in the majority. Shiites recognize the authority of the descendants of Ali, whom they give the title of imam. The imam is their most important leader and spiritual guide.

A small number of Egyptian Muslims are Sufis, who seek to approach unity with God through mystical methods. Many Sufis give up all their belongings and all forms of pleasure. Through rituals involving dance and music they enter a trance-like state that, they believe, brings them closer to God.

All followers of Islam are expected to observe five duties. These duties are called the Five Pillars of Islam. The first duty is the profession of faith (*shahadah*): "I testify that there is no God but God. I testify that Muhammad is the prophet of God." Muslims must recite this at least once in their life, and believe fully in it. The second duty is prayer (*salat*). Muslims are to pray five times a day, facing in the direction of their holy city of Mecca. They memorize and chant prayers from the Qur'an. The third duty is **fasting** (*sawm*). Muslims fast from sunrise to sunset during the holy month of Ramadan. The timing of Ramadan varies, depending on the phases of the moon. During the fast, believers are to reflect on their faith and be purified. The fourth duty is the paying of the tax (*zakat*). This is a tax of about 2.5 percent on the goods and earnings of a believer. The tax is meant to help the poor members of society and to make Muslims less attached to material possessions. The fifth duty is pilgrimage (*hajj*). If at all possible, every Muslim is supposed to go to Mecca, in modern-day Saudi Arabia, at least once in his or her life. There, in the birthplace of Muhammad, the pilgrims perform special rituals at the most important Muslim shrine, the Ka'bah.

Islam touches every aspect of life in Egypt. Most Egyptian Muslims are very religious. Traditionally, they greet each other by asking that the peace and mercy of God come upon the other person. They believe in the importance of strong families and obedience to the government. Most Muslims reject the ideas of fundamentalist groups who practice terrorism and try to overthrow governments. But in Egypt, as in certain other Muslim societies, the freedom of women is limited in many respects. They pray and perform other activities separately from men.

One way in which Islam in Egypt differs from the way the religion is practiced in other countries is the reverence Egyptians show toward the dead. This custom is probably related to the traditions surrounding death in the religion of the ancient Egyptians. Outside of the big cities, many small communities have their own saint. The saint's tomb is a sacred place. Many people also believe in the use of magic, spells, and potions. These beliefs are not a part of Islam but come from the traditional religions of the Egyptians.

Egypt's largest Christian church is the Coptic Church, practiced by 9 percent of Egyptians. The word *Coptic* comes from the Greek word for "Egyptian." Christianity first became an important Egyptian religion in the first century CE, during Roman rule. Egyptian Christianity soon developed its own traditions. Around the year 450, the Coptic Church separated from the other churches of the Roman Empire, including the Roman Catholic Church. The main reason for the split was the Copts' belief that Jesus Christ's nature was always completely divine. Other churches believed that Christ was both human and divine when he was on earth. Since the split, the Copts have suffered oppression on and off for hundreds of years. In their early history, the Copts faced persecution from other Christian churches. Some Muslim rulers allowed the Copts to worship freely. Others tried to stop their activity. Although modern Copts are involved in politics, they prefer to see Egypt as an independent and prosperous nation rather than as part of the Arab world. This attitude has made them a target for Islamic fundamentalist groups in recent years. Outside of Egypt, a few Coptic churches exist in places such as Jerusalem and Sudan. The Coptic Church has its own pope, also called the patriarch. The patriarch lives in Alexandria, the church's main center.

In their church services, the Copts make some use of the Coptic language, which comes from a form of the ancient Egyptian language but was also influenced by Greek. However, Arabic is the main language of the Coptic Church today.

Most Christians in Egypt today are Copts, but Catholics, members of the Greek Orthodox Church, and some Protestants are found in small numbers, as are Jews. In the past, there used to be more members of these other religions. Now, many of them have left the country and moved to other parts of the world.

 ## Text-Dependent Questions

1. When did Hosni Mubarak step down as president of Egypt?
2. How did Sadat's infitah help the Egyptian economy?
3. What is one difference between Sunni and Shiite Muslims?

 ## Research Project

Imagine you are an Egyptian government official at the time the Aswan High Dam was proposed. Using the Internet or your school library, research the history of the Aswan High Dam and make a chart listing the pros and cons of the building project

A man reads in Memphis, the ancient capital of Egypt, which is located south of present-day Cairo. For development efforts to succeed, Egypt must confront major problems with its educational system; fewer than three-fourths of all Egyptians over the age of 15 can read and write.

The People

Egypt has been influenced by a wide array of cultures and includes people from a variety of racial backgrounds. However, most Egyptians today are Arabs, descendants of people originally from the Arabian Peninsula. Within the Arab population, Bedouins make up a distinct group. These desert dwellers were traditionally nomads—that is, they wandered from place to place—but today they are more likely to remain in one place. That is because much of the land over which they used to roam is controlled by the government or used to cultivate food.

Among Egyptians of African descent, the Nubians make up the largest group. Originally, the Nubians came from southern Egypt and the northern Sudan. Many were displaced by the construction of the Aswan High Dam. Other African groups include the Sa'idi, the Beja, and the Berbers. Though Muslims, the Berbers do not speak the Arabic language. They live in the mountains and deserts of all the North African countries.

Egypt's inhabitants also include descendants of Persians, Greeks, Romans, and Turks. Some people from Italy, France, and other countries live in Egypt, though these foreign communities are relatively small.

LANGUAGES

Arabic is the official language of Egypt. But the language can be used differently, depending on the situation. A formal version of Arabic, associated with Cairo, is used in television, movies, and radio broadcasts. This form is also widely used in other parts of the Arab world. The Arabic used in everyday conversation is more casual. People who live in different parts of the country speak different kinds of Arabic. An Arabic-speaking desert dweller would have a hard time understanding an Arabic speaker from a big city such as Cairo or Alexandria. Classical Arabic, the language of the Qur'an, is used in religious services. The modern written form of Arabic, used in literature and other areas, has developed from Classical Arabic.

Other languages exist in Egypt. The Nubians, the Berbers, and the Beja all have their own African languages. In addition, because of Egypt's popularity as a tourist destination, many Egyptians speak some English, French, or other European or Asian languages.

THE FAMILY

Family life is one of the cornerstones of Egyptian society. As a rule, Egyptian families are more structured and close-knit than

Word to Understand in This Chapter

bazaar—a market in the Eastern world where a wide variety of goods are sold.

A farmer and his children enjoy a breakfast of flat bread in their village near Cairo. Though there have been some changes over the past century, traditional family life remains the norm in Egypt.

Western families, with each member expected to fulfill a given role. However, economic and social changes over the past century have brought some changes to family life, especially for young workers.

At the head of the Egyptian family is the husband and father. He is expected to provide for his family and to ensure that the other members of the household bring honor to the family.

The wife and mother makes sure that the household runs smoothly. This can include everything from cooking and cleaning to running a family business. She is mainly responsible for bringing up the children.

Marriage is the basis for family life. It is rare for an Egyptian man or woman to choose not to get married. Nothing is more important in an Egyptian family than having children. Boys are especially valued, though girls are also loved and cherished. Most families hope to have at least two boys.

In the traditional Egyptian family, adult children of either sex rarely leave their parents' household before getting married. And a young woman is viewed as being under her father's authority until

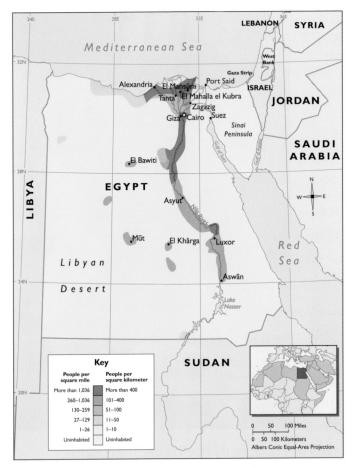

This map shows the distribution of population in Egypt. Much of the large country is sparsely populated, with the majority of Egypt's nearly 86 million people living along the Nile River and delta. There are a few pockets of heavier population in the center of the country.

she marries, at which point she comes under the authority of her husband. Egyptian views of marriage mean that it is much easier for a man to divorce a woman than for a woman to divorce a man. Although women are still restricted in many ways, some things are changing. During the 1990s, several conferences took place in Egypt on the rights and roles of women.

Usually, a young couple live near the household of the man's parents. If they cannot afford to have their own house or apartment, they may live with the man's parents. Sometimes an entire extended family lives together, including grandparents, nieces and nephews, and relatives by marriage. They may live in the same house or apartment building, or at a short distance from one another in their town or village. Young men may leave home to find work, but they are still viewed as part of the household. Although men make up most of the workforce, today it is much more common than previously for women to work in industry and service jobs.

The type and size of housing in Egypt depends on where the housing is located. The big cities are crowded with high-rises and apartment buildings. Wealthier people live in houses. Egypt's rapidly growing population has led to a severe housing shortage in cities such as Cairo and Alexandria. Some people have to build huts on top of apartment buildings, or on any spare piece of land that they can find. Some people live among the ancient tombs outside Cairo. In the countryside, villagers build houses from mud bricks and plaster. Under the rule of Anwar el-Sadat, electricity was introduced into most parts of Egypt. This means that many people in even the most remote villages can watch TV.

CLOTHING AND FASHION

Styles of dress and grooming in Egypt have been influenced by the climate, tradition, fashion, and even religious customs. On the streets of the large Egyptian cities today, people sporting European and American styles of clothing walk side by side with people wearing traditional clothing of a kind that has been worn for hundreds of years.

The most popular item of traditional clothing is the *galabeya*. Men and women wear this loose, long-sleeved cotton robe. Although it falls to the ankles, the *galabeya* is a cool and comfortable garment for the Egyptian climate. It is also considered modest, which is important for a woman's garment. Men usually wear white, blue, gray, or another sober color. Women are more likely to wear bright colors. In the cities, women may also wear fashions from Europe and America, though they do not usually wear pants. Blue jeans are popular among men, and many businessmen wear suits.

As in other parts of the Arab world, many Egyptian women wear a veil. This is a tradition associated with Islam, though it may have started before the religion's founding. Egyptian women do not have to wear a veil, but many choose to do so. Some veils are wrapped around the head, covering the hair but showing the whole face. Others cover the whole face, with only a small gap for the eyes. This type of veil is less common today. Egyptian women do not view the veil as an oppressive tradition. They wear it to show that they are serious about their religion, because it simplifies their beauty routines, or because so many other women wear it and they would prefer to fit in.

EGYPTIAN CUISINE

The people of Egypt enjoy a wide variety of foods, from simple breads and bean dishes to delicious chicken and fish recipes. Bread and beans have been two of the most important foods in the Egyptian diet for thousands of years. *Fuul* is a popular dish that combines boiled and mashed beans with onions, tomatoes, lemon, and other ingredients. Beans also appear in salads and as fried sandwich fillings. Breads include flat bread and French-style bread. The Egyptians do not always eat meat, but favorites include lamb, chicken, and pigeon. They often serve meat when guests are present. This custom shows generosity to the guests, since meat dishes are more expensive than vegetarian dishes.

An Egyptian meal often starts with several small dishes, called *mezze*. These dishes may include salads, dips, olives, pickled vegetables, and similar foods. Main courses include meat casseroles, lamb and rice meatballs, and stuffed vegetables. Grilled fish is especially popular in coastal areas. For dessert, Egyptians enjoy puddings and pastries with nuts, raisins, and honey. Fruit, both dried and fresh, is also a common dessert.

Tea served with sugar and without milk is a favorite hot drink, as is strong Turkish coffee served in small cups. Another popular hot drink is made of arrowroot, cinnamon, and nuts. Egyptian cold drinks include a wide variety of fruit juices, and a more limited variety of alcoholic beverages, mostly beer and wine. Muslims are not

This Egyptian man is wearing the traditional cotton *galabeya*. In the cities, Egyptians are just as likely to wear Western clothing as traditional dress.

supposed to drink alcohol, and Egyptian alcohol is not highly regarded.

EDUCATION

Education has not always been a right in Egypt. Even now, when all children are expected to attend elementary school for a few years at least, not all of them are actually able to attend. Still, much has improved in the educational system, especially for girls and women.

Before the rule of the Ottoman officer Muhammad Ali in the 19th century, all schools were run by religious authorities. Muhammad Ali modernized the educational system and made it more accessible. His wife even founded a school for girls. When Egypt became a republic in the 1950s, the new government spent large sums of money on the creation of new schools. The enrollment of children in schools doubled more than once in the decades that followed, although it slowed down again in the 1980s.

Today, all children between the ages of 6 and 14 are supposed to go to school. In practice, children must attend only until the age of 12. But even in this age group, there are many children who do not go to school at all. Others go for only a short time. One reason for this is that children are needed to work at home and in family businesses. In rural areas and poorer communities, families may choose to educate just one or two children, at the most.

The Egyptian school system suffers from a lack of teachers. In addition, many schools are ill equipped and too small. Because of these problems and a lack of access to education among many Egyptians, half the population cannot read or write.

Among children who finish elementary school at the age of 12, only about half go on to further schooling. Preparatory school, the next step, lasts for three years. If the student passes the exam at the end of this time, he or she may go to high school. Depending on how well they do in the final exams at the end of high school, stu-

 Quick Facts: The People of Egypt

Population: 86,895,099 (rank 16th in the world).
Ethnic groups: Egyptian 99.6%, other 0.4% (2006 census).
Religions: Muslim (predominantly Sunni) 90%, Christian (majority Coptic Orthodox, other Christians include Armenian Apostolic, Catholic, Maronite, Orthodox, and Anglican) 10% (2012).
Language: Arabic (official), English and French widely understood by educated classes.
Age structure:
    0–14 years: 32.1%
    15–24 years: 17.8%
    25–54 years: 38.4%
    55–64 years: 6.7%
    65 years and over: 5%
Population growth rate: 1.84% (rank 64th in the world).
Birth rate: 23.35 births/1,000 population (rank 68th in the world).
Death rate: 4.77 deaths/1,000 population (rank 196th in the world).
Infant mortality rate: 22.41 deaths/ 1,000 live births (rank 80th in the world).
Life expectancy at birth: 73.45 years (rank 123rd in the world).
Literacy: 73.9% (2012).

All figures are 2014 estimates unless otherwise indicated.
Source: Adapted from CIA World Factbook, 2015.

dents are allowed to sign up for different kinds of post-secondary training.

Among families who can afford it, many young people receive a university education. This group now includes many women, who can get jobs in science, politics, and other fields. Higher education is provided by 20 private and public colleges and universities in Egypt.

THE ARTS, MUSIC, AND ENTERTAINMENT

Egypt is recognized in the Arab world as a leader in the area of arts and entertainment. In film, television, music, visual arts, and literature, the people of Egypt combine Western ideas and influences with their own culture and traditions. The accomplishments of Egyptian filmmakers, musicians, artists, and writers are enjoyed all over the world.

Egypt is the only Arab country that produces a significant number of movies. The first Egyptian films started to appear in the late 1920s, and a huge number have been released since then. The most famous Egyptian film director is Youssef Chahine, who directed films for well over 50 years. His films include *Cairo Station* (1958), *Alexandria, Why?* (1978), and *Destiny* (1997). Their subjects range from love stories to criticisms of religious fundamentalism. Some of his films take place in modern-day Egypt, while others are set in the distant past. The famous Egyptian actor Omar Sharif appeared in films by Chahine, as well as in American movies. Although he has made only one film—*The Night of Counting the Years* (1969)—Shadi Abdelsalam is regarded as another important Egyptian director. His film, set in the 1880s, is about the discovery of ancient royal graves by grave-robbers. It is also seen as a commentary on the political situation in Egypt at the time of the movie's release. Attyat El Abnoudy has concentrated on documentaries about Egyptian women. Her films have won many awards.

Television is available to people even in remote parts of Egypt. Series such as *The White Flag*, which appeared in the late 1980s, have become widely known and discussed by people across Egypt. *The White Flag* concerns the struggle between the owner of a famous villa and a greedy real estate developer who threatens to demolish it. However, the most famous TV programs are those that make up the annual Ramadan *Fawazir*. The original *Fawazir* were riddles written to entertain people after sundown during the month of Ramadan. Today, the *Fawazir* consist of game shows that offer contestants the opportunity to send in the answers to daily riddles and win prizes such as cars and holidays.

Egyptians perform and listen to a wide variety of musical styles. In rural areas, people continue to play the same type of music that their ancestors enjoyed. Traditional music often tells a story. It may also be related to a religious observance or festival. The performance of this music may involve just a few instruments: a two-sided drum, stringed instruments like the banjo and the viol, and simple hand-clapping.

During the 20th century, musicians in Egypt's cities combined traditional influences with a more Western style of popular music. Umm Kalthoum, who was very popular in the 1960s, performed her songs of love and loss in the classical Arabic style. She sang in a distinctive warbling style, using musical scales that rose and fell dramatically. Her songs were backed up by huge orchestras and choirs. Muhammad Abd al-Wahhab became famous for his work with a musical style called *takht*, which originally used only a few instruments. In songs such as "The Eternal River" and "The Gondola," Abd al-Wahhab used a large number of European instruments in an Egyptian style. The result was a combination of Western, Arabic, classical, and popular influences. After Abd al-Wahhab's death, one critic called his work "the most sincere expression of all tendencies and composers" in Egyptian music.

The music heard in dance clubs and on the radio uses fast dance beats, synthesizers, and other elements from Western pop music. Most popular Egyptian music falls into two categories: *shaabi* ("people") music, and *al-Jeel* ("the generation") music. *Shaabi* is associated with Ahmed Adawiya, who developed this style in the 1970s. It uses traditional rhythms, but with a modern sound and at a modern speed. The lyrics use the language and popular expressions of the working classes. Some of the lyrics are about love or about dancing the night away, while others deal with social or political problems. In one of Ahmed Adawiya's songs, he sings sadly: "How crowded is the world/Crowded and friends lose their way/Crowded and merciless/A free-for-all." *Al-Jeel* music has a more electronic sound, though it also uses traditional sounds and rhythms. Singers such as Ehab Tawfek sing about love, staying away from controversial subjects. Still, the differences between these two styles are not always clear. Currently, one of the most popular Egyptian singers is Amr Diab. His songs, sung in both Arabic and English, have become popular all over the world.

Twentieth-century Egyptian visual art came from a combination of modern Western styles and the art of the distant past. A group called the Neo-Pharaonists used ancient Egyptian styles of art as a basis for something new. Muhammad Nagy is viewed as the founder of modern Egyptian painting. Around 1910, he studied under the famous French painter Claude Monet. Nagy's paintings combine modern European painting with Egyptian themes, colors, and patterns. Hamid Nada was a member of the Contemporary Egyptian Art Group, founded in the 1940s. Some of his works are like the art of the ancient Egyptians, both in style and in subject. One of his most famous paintings, *Working in the Field*, looks almost like a child's drawing of peasants and donkeys.

Egypt has produced many writers who are popular throughout the Arab world and in other countries. The novelist Naguib Mahfouz

A street musician in Esna holds his *kamancheh*, a traditional spiked fiddle of Persian origin that is an ancestor to many modern bowed instruments, such as the violin. The instrument is played vertically; it has a conical neck with a hollowed bulb at the bottom made of walnut or mulberry wood and covered with stretched skin.

won the Nobel Prize in literature in 1988. He was the first Arabic writer to win this honor. In awarding him the Nobel Prize, the Swedish Academy of Letters called his writing "an Arabic narrative art that applies to all mankind." Mahfouz has written more than 30 novels, as well as collections of short stories. Some of his novels take place in ancient Egypt. Others, like the Cairo Trilogy, are set in modern times. Many of his works are about the problem of social inequality. Tawfik al-Hakim has written plays, biography, novels, philosophy, and fictional conversations between real and imaginary people. His essay *The Prison of Life* is about the first 30 years of his own life. Presidents Nasser and Sadat gave al-Hakim special awards for the work he did to help Egyptian theater. Egypt has also inspired many of its authors to write poetry. Early in the 20th century, the poet Hafiz Ibrahim wrote a famous poem called "Egypt Speaks for Herself." The singer Umm Kalthoum later performed this poem. C.

P. Cavafy was a writer of Greek descent who spent most of his life in Egypt. He wrote poetry in Greek about his city, Alexandria.

FRIENDSHIP AND HOSPITALITY

The average Egyptian works very hard without earning a great deal of money. Still, Egyptians find many ways to enjoy themselves. They like to watch and play sports such as soccer and field hockey. In street cafés and coffeehouses, men gather to smoke, read, and talk. They can also listen to live music and play games such as cards and dominoes. **Bazaars** are a great place to shop, meet friends, and exchange news.

Foreign visitors find that the Egyptians are a warm and friendly people. They value their families and their friendships very deeply, and they are happy to share their country with those who are new to it. Egyptians who are looking after a guest often insist on paying for everything for their visitor. Western visitors may find that if they admire an item of jewelry or something else belonging to their Egyptian friend, the Egyptian may offer it to them to show generosity. These customs can be surprising to us, but to the Egyptians, they are a normal part of hospitality and their way of life.

 Text-Dependent Questions

1. The form of Arabic associated with what city is used throughout the Arab world?
2. What are mezze?

 Research Project

Egyptian actor Omar Sharif gained worldwide fame. Use the Internet or your school library to research his life and write a brief biography that includes information on how he was received in Hollywood. If possible, watch one of his films.

Dusk falls over the brightly lit streets and skyline of Alexandria, Egypt's second-largest city, which was founded in the fourth century BCE by Alexander the Great and may contain the ancient conquerer's tomb. Today about 43 percent of Egypt's population lives in urban areas.

Communities

Egypt is a fascinating land where the 21st century CE mingles with the 21st century BCE. Many of Egypt's bustling cities of today—modern centers of business, industry, and tourism—served, in ancient times, as capitals for pharaohs, centers of trade and commerce, or important places of worship.

CAIRO

Located at the southernmost point of the Nile delta, Cairo is not only the largest city in Egypt, but also the largest in Africa. It has a population of 17 to 22 million, including its suburbs. Cairo's name comes from Al-Qahirah, meaning "The Victorious" or "The Conqueror." This name goes back to the conquest of Egypt by the Muslim Fatimid dynasty in 969 CE. Cairo has also been called Umm Dunya, or "Mother of the World." Egyptians usually call the city Misr, which is also a name for all of Egypt.

In the time of the pharaohs, the major communities in the Cairo area were at Memphis and Giza. The pharaohs ruled out of Memphis and worshiped at its temples; they built their great pyramids at Giza. Today, Memphis is a ruin, and Giza is a suburb of Cairo. About 2000 years ago, the Romans built a fort on the site. But the first major settlement was Fustat, built in 641 CE by the conquering Muslim forces. A mosque dating back to the time of the conquest still stands in Cairo, though it has been altered many times. The Fatimid conquerors started the city as we know it today. They built Al-Azhar University, the world's most important center of Muslim learning and considered the oldest university in the world. Its main subjects are still the Islamic religion and the Arabic language, although students can now take other courses as well.

The Fatimids were followed by many other conquerors. Other Muslim dynasties, the Mamluks, the Ottoman Turks, the French, and the British added to the city. Today, the different areas of the city built by various civilizations still have their own character and architecture.

Central Cairo, on the eastern side of the Nile, is quite modern, with many businesses, hotels, and expensive residences. Old Cairo, also known as Coptic Cairo, is located in the south of the city and is the center of the Coptic Christian religion in Cairo. Its buildings include the remains of the original Roman settlement. Islamic Cairo, to the east, has mosques from all periods of Muslim rule. Because of the tall, elegant towers of these mosques, Cairo is sometimes called "the City of a Thousand Minarets." The Citadel, to the south of Islamic Cairo, has been a military area for hundreds of years. The legendary Muslim ruler Saladin began construction of the Citadel, and for many centuries after, the rulers of Egypt lived there. The most famous building in this area is the Muhammad Ali Mosque, built in the mid-19th century. Its style is Turkish, with richly decorated domes. To the south and east of Cairo lie the Cities of the Dead. These ancient cemeteries have always been inhabited

The Nile River runs through Cairo, the largest city in Egypt.

by people who cannot afford to live elsewhere, and today hundreds of thousands of Egyptians have established shops and places to live among the tombs. Many of them actually live in the mausoleums, or aboveground tombs, built for the dead. Although this is not an easy existence, the cemetery dwellers do not necessarily live unhappy lives. In his book *Cairo: The City Victorious*, author Max Rodenbeck spoke to an elderly man living in the Cities of the Dead, who said: "Of course I am happy. . . . I live in the greatest city in the world."

Giza, to the southwest of Cairo, lies on the western bank of the

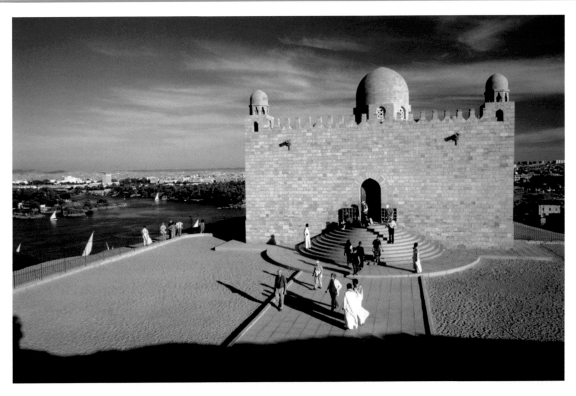

Visitors outside the mausoleum of the Aga Khan III, on the west bank of the Nile River near the Aswan Dam. The Aga Khan was the spiritual leader of the Ismailis, a sect of Shiite Muslims. The mausoleum was built after his death in 1957.

Muslim armies took Alexandria in 641 CE. The conquest of this important city made them the supreme rulers of Egypt. However, they did not continue to rule out of Alexandria. Though still an important trading center, the city declined over hundreds of years.

Muhammad Ali worked to revive Alexandria in the early 1800s. The French and the British also added to Alexandria and helped to restore it to prominence. Many foreigners, especially Greeks, Italians, and Jews, moved into the city. Today, however, there are far fewer people from other countries, and Alexandria has lost much of its international flavor.

The city is about 12 miles (19 km) long from east to west. A popular walking area called the Corniche runs around the curve of the Eastern Harbor. The Fort of Qaytbay, which is more than 500 years old, stands on one side of the harbor where the Pharos lighthouse used to be. Remains of the lighthouse, as well as remains of what may be Cleopatra's palace, have been found underwater. Two streets from ancient times, the Canopic Way and the Street of the Soma, run through Alexandria. The tomb of Alexander may have been at the crossroads of these two streets. Some of the most important Greek and Roman monuments, like the Roman Theater, are located on or near these streets. In the southwestern part of the city, there is a large area of underground tombs built by the Romans. The architecture of these tombs combines Egyptian and Roman styles.

Alexandria's economy is similar to Cairo's. Many people work in banking, and textile production is also important. And Alexandria is still a working port that ships grain, textiles, fruit, and other Egyptian products to other parts of the world.

ASWAN

Aswan is the southernmost of Egypt's major cities. Its population of around 266,000 is exceeded by at least a dozen other Egyptian cities, but Aswan has an importance that goes beyond size. It connects Egypt to Sudan and other countries to the south. Because of its position, its character is more African than Egypt's other cities.

The modern city of Aswan lies on the eastern bank of the Nile. Elephantine Island, next to Aswan in the middle of the Nile, has been inhabited for thousands of years. It was the site of an ancient town called Yeb, a trading post and religious center. The Egyptians believed that the source of the Nile was nearby, and a fortress at Yeb protected Egypt from invaders traveling north along the river. The Romans also used this site as a military outpost, and, much later, so did the British.

Today, Aswan is still a center for trade with Sudan. Its factories produce copper, steel, and cement. Much of the energy for these factories comes from the nearby Aswan High Dam. A fishing industry has developed on Lake Nasser, which was created by the Aswan High Dam. Aswan attracts many tourists because of its restful atmosphere and its unique culture.

PORT SAID

Located on the Mediterranean Sea, at the northern end of the Suez Canal, Port Said is one of Egypt's newer cities. It was founded in 1859, when the canal was being built. With a population of more than 570,000, it ranks behind only Cairo, urban areas in the Cairo metropolitan area, and Alexandria among Egypt's largest cities.

After the opening of the Suez Canal, Port Said became one of the world's major centers for trade. Coal shipments, as well as cotton, rice, and many other products, passed through Port Said and the canal. The city also became known for illegal activities, especially the exchange of drugs. Much of the city was damaged or destroyed during the Suez Crisis of 1956.

Today, Port Said is a stopping place for cruise ships, a tourist resort, and a tax-free zone. Its main industries, besides shipping, include textiles, glass, and car batteries. It also has a large number of computer and publishing companies.

EGYPTIAN CELEBRATIONS

The people of Egypt celebrate a large number of holidays and festivals. Some of these celebrations are national, some local. The religious holidays of Egypt's Islamic majority are the same celebrated all over the Arab world. Coptic Christians, of course, have a different set of religious holidays. Some celebrations combine Islamic and Christian traditions with aspects of the religion of the ancient Egyptians.

Dervishes perform the Tannura, a sacred meditative form of dance, outside the Ghuriya complex in Old Cairo. For more than 700 years Muslim mystics called Sufis have made the dance, which involves great training and concentration, a part of their religious devotions. Today the Tannura's continuous whirls and colorful flaring skirts may just as likely represent simple entertainment.

The Islamic calendar is based on lunar cycles—each month begins when the crescent moon first becomes visible to a human observer after a new moon. Because the Islamic year is slightly longer than 354 days, Muslim holidays shift back with respect to the Gregorian, or Western, calendar about 11 days each year. For example, the Islamic New Year fell on January 10 in 2008 (the year 1429 in the Islamic calendar, which begins with 622 CE), but in 2015 (1436 in the Islamic calendar) it fell on October 13.

The most important Muslim observance is Ramadan, the ninth month of the Islamic calendar and the time when Muhammad first began receiving the Qur'an. From sunrise to sunset every day, Muslims do not eat, drink, or smoke. They often spend extra time in prayer and study of the Qur'an. In the evening, they celebrate and enjoy themselves by eating special foods, playing music, and visiting with family and friends. According to the Qur'an, Muslims can "eat and drink until the whiteness of the day becomes distinct from the blackness of the night at dawn, then complete the fast till night." In Egypt, the Ramadan *Fawazir* shows are a very popular part of Ramadan. These TV shows involve the telling of a riddle every evening. There are many prizes to be won, but everyone enjoys the singing, dancing, and other entertainment in the shows. At the end of Ramadan, Muslims celebrate Eid al-Fitr, or the Feast of Fast Breaking. During this three-day celebration friends and families gather for prayers and special meals. In Cairo, Eid al-Fitr turns into a particularly large celebration.

Egyptian Muslims observe several other special days throughout the year. Eid al-Adha, the Feast of Sacrifice, takes place in the Islamic month of Dhu'l-Hijja. It commemorates the willingness of the patriarch Abraham (Ibrahim) to sacrifice his son. This is a time when families slaughter and eat a sheep, to remember that God provided Abraham with a sheep to sacrifice instead of his son. For many poor Egyptians, this is the only time during the year when they can afford to eat meat. Another special day is Ras el-Sana el-Hegira, which marks the beginning of the Muslim New Year.

Coptic Christians celebrate Christmas and Easter, like other Christian churches around the world. They celebrate Christmas on January 7, the date used by the Eastern Orthodox Church. Copts fast before Easter and at other times during the year.

The custom of the *moulid* is shared by most Egyptians, whether they are Muslims or Christians. The *moulid*, which combines several religious traditions, is a celebration dedicated to the memory of a holy man or woman. The custom is found only in

Egypt. *Moulids* take place year-round and may last for a few days or up to a week. The most important is the Moulid al-Nabi, which takes place in August and commemorates the birthday of Muhammad, the founder of Islam. Many towns have processions for this celebration. People come from all over for the huge procession in Cairo. The *moulid* of Abu

The interior of a Coptic church at Sharm el-Sheik, on the Sinai Peninsula.

Haggag at Luxor continues a tradition that has gone on for thousands of years. People honor the ancient gods of Luxor by carrying a boat around the temple. Coptic Christians and Jews also have a few *moulids* of their own. All *moulids* include street fairs, wild dancing by Sufi mystics, performances by trained animals, and loud music.

 ## Text-Dependent Questions

1. What is a Nilometer?
2. Where is Tahrir Square?
3. What is a moulid?

 ## Research Project

It is believed that the library at Alexandria burned in the 4th century but there are differing accounts as to how and why is burned. Use the Internet or your school library to investigate different accounts of what happened to this ancient library. Which version do you think is the most likely?

Election posters promote candidates for a parliamentary election in Cairo, January 2012. The parliament elected after Mubarak's reign ended was dissolved when Egypt's supreme court ruled that the election had violated the constitution. Elections for a new parliament were scheduled to be held in 2015, but were delayed several times.

Foreign Relations

For thousands of years Egypt occupied a strategic position in the world, and Egyptians found their land coveted by a succession of invaders. Egypt remains strategically important in the 21st century. And, as has occurred at several points in its history, in its foreign relations the nation finds itself pulled in different directions. While Egypt is a leader in the Arab world, the country has also allied itself with the United States since the 1970s, and has had relations, though not always **cordial**, with Israel. Finally, though Egypt's political, cultural, and ethnic character is distinctly Arab, most of its territory lies in Africa. Because of its size and economic importance relative to the rest of the continent, Egypt has been expected to assume a leadership role in African affairs.

FOREIGN AFFAIRS UNDER THE BRITISH

Egypt was under British control from the late 1800s until the country became a republic in 1953. This meant that Britain made the key decisions about Egypt's relations with other nations. In 1888, Britain and other powerful nations such as Germany, France, Italy, and Russia signed the Constantinople Convention of the Suez Canal. The convention guaranteed that the Suez Canal would stay open at all times, even if war broke out. Egypt itself was not really part of the convention, though the Egyptian ruler was expected to cooperate with the decision.

During the First World War, Britain decided what Egypt's place in the war would be. Officially, Egypt had been under the rule of the Ottoman Empire. Because the Ottoman Empire was an ally of its primary enemy, Germany, Britain officially took control of Egypt and used the country as a military center during the war. By the time of the Second World War, Egypt was technically independent, but the British continued to exert influence and maintain a significant military presence there. Full autonomy after the war brought a new set of challenges. Events such as the Suez Crisis of 1956 showed the strain in Egypt's foreign relations, as Britain and France united with Israel against the Egyptian takeover of the Suez Canal.

THE ARAB LEAGUE AND THE CONFLICT WITH ISRAEL

In 1945 an event took place that would prove pivotal to Egypt's foreign relations: the formation of the Arab League. The Arab League, which now consists of 22 member nations, was founded to foster economic, political, and cultural ties among Arab countries.

 Words to Understand in This Chapter

cordial—warm and friendly.
Islamist—espousing radically fundamentalist Islamic doctrine that is usually hostile to Western societies and ideas.

Frequently the league and Western nations have experienced strained relations. And sometimes a member of the league has found itself at odds with the other members. This has been particularly true of Egypt, one of the most powerful and influential nations in the Arab world and a country the other Arab states look toward to take a lead in promoting their interests. The most divisive issue has been Israel.

In 1948, the United Nations partitioned Palestine and created the State of Israel. The members of the Arab League refused to accept the UN decision, and Egypt, along with Iraq, Syria, Lebanon, and Jordan, attacked the new Jewish state. Israel managed to beat back the Arab attackers and the UN eventually brokered an end to the fighting. Still, tensions between the Arabs and the Israelis remained.

 Did You Know?

Egypt, which is first and foremost an Arab nation, is also a leader in the African Union (AU). This international organization promotes economic development and cooperation among nations on the continent of Africa.

In 1964, at meetings held in Cairo, the Arab nations created the Palestine Liberation Organization (PLO) in order to unify Palestinian efforts to destroy Israel and create a Palestinian Arab country in its place. (As a result of the 1948 Arab-Israeli war, the Palestinians had lost all the land given to them in the UN partition. Israel had taken some of it, and Jordan and Egypt the rest: Jordan occupied the West Bank area, and Egypt took Gaza.) Initially, the Arab League nations believed they could control the PLO's activities and probably intended to use the organization as an instrument of their own foreign policy. But the PLO came under the leadership of Yasir Arafat and over the years became increasingly independent. Eventually it would become a full member of the Arab League and win recognition by the UN. Its early activities, however, were largely confined to cross-border incursions into Israel and acts of terrorism.

The activities of the PLO—a group supported by the Arab League—contributed to the tensions that led to the Six-Day War of 1967. That conflict began when Israel launched a preemptive strike against Egypt, Jordan, and Syria, which were preparing to go to war against the Jewish state. It turned into an utter rout of the Arab nations.

SADAT EXTENDS AN OLIVE BRANCH

At first Anwar el-Sadat, who became Egypt's president in 1970, continued his country's warlike policies toward Israel. In 1973 Egypt and Syria jointly launched the so-called October War against Israel, which ended inconclusively. But the essential purpose of the war was achieved as it enabled Egypt to begin a new relationship with the United States, and, through Washington, to pressure Israel. After four years of partially successful diplomacy, Sadat told Egypt's People's Assembly that he was willing to go anywhere—even Jerusalem—to bring an end to the decades of hostility. And on November 20, 1977, he appeared before the Israeli legislature, the Knesset, and declared, "I come to you today on solid ground to shape a new life and to establish peace. We all love this land, the land of God, we all, Moslems, Christians and Jews, all worship God." With the help of mediation by U.S. president Jimmy Carter, the diplomatic opening paid off. In 1978 Sadat and Israel's prime minister, Menachem Begin, accepted a peace agreement, the Camp David Accords. The following year the peace treaty was signed, officially ending the state of war between Egypt and Israel.

The peace treaty brought tangible benefits to Egypt. It removed the constant threat of war with a powerful neighbor and freed the Egyptian economy from the necessity of continually focusing on military expenditures. And it increased Egypt's status among Western nations, which believed that the Middle East—and the world—was now a safer place. It also paved the way for substantial

In 1978, U.S. president Jimmy Carter helped negotiate a treaty between Egypt and Israel; known as the Camp David Accords because the terms were hashed out at the presidential retreat in Camp David, Maryland, the agreement is still in force today. Sadat, Carter, and Israeli prime minister Menachem Begin signed the agreement in 1979. The accords angered the rest of the Arab world; Egypt was expelled from the Arab League and not readmitted until 1989.

U.S. aid and greater trade opportunities with America. The United States has funded projects related to power generation, transportation, water systems, and other areas, and it has also provided modern military equipment to Egypt.

Yet in the Arab world the response to the peace treaty with Israel was one of near-universal outrage. The other Arab nations believed that Egypt had betrayed them in pursuing a separate peace with Israel. And the PLO, along with most ordinary Palestinians, felt that Egypt had abandoned their cause, even though the agreement called for Israel to allow Palestinians to have their own government. Boutros Boutros-Ghali, Sadat's minister of state for foreign affairs, later revealed in his autobiography: "What [the Arab world] feared was that behind the treaty might be a secret alliance between Israel and Egypt, with the backing of the United States. . . . The military power of Egypt and Israel together would be more than any combination of Arab states could contemplate confronting." The Arab League expelled Egypt. When Sadat was assassinated in 1981, only three member nations of the Arab League sent representatives to his funeral.

MENDING FENCES

Sadat's successor, Hosni Mubarak, worked to rebuild relations with the other Arab countries while respecting the terms of the Egypt-Israel peace treaty and maintaining close ties to the United States and the West. During the Iran-Iraq war of the 1980s, Mubarak offered Egyptian assistance to oil-exporting Arab countries, whose economies were threatened by the disruption in tanker traffic through the Persian Gulf. In return, Egypt received much-needed financial aid, and in 1989 the Arab League readmitted Egypt as a member. The Arab League headquarters returned to Cairo.

Egypt proved to be a steady ally of the United States during the 1991 Persian Gulf War, which was precipitated by Iraq's 1990 invasion of its southern neighbor Kuwait. Though both Iraq and Kuwait are Arab countries, Egypt—like most other Arab nations—supported the UN resolution that authorized the use of force to drive Iraq out of Kuwait, and it joined the U.S.-led coalition that accomplished that. Egypt's contingent of 35,000 troops constituted one of the largest in the coalition, which decisively won the brief war.

After the war, Egypt signed a treaty with other Arab nations to help stabilize the situation in the Persian Gulf area. In 1991 Egypt also participated in the Madrid Peace Conference—which brought together Israeli, Syrian, Lebanese, Jordanian, and Palestinian representatives under American and Russian chairmanship. The purpose was to work toward peace agreements between Israel and its longtime Arab adversaries. The conference led to a treaty between Jordan and Israel, as well as the so-called Oslo peace process involving the Palestinians and Israelis, but the effort to conclusively settle all Mideast hostilities fell short.

NEW CRISES

By 2000 tensions in the region were boiling over into violence once again. Seven years earlier, Israel and the PLO had finally seemed to be on the road to peace when they signed the Oslo Accords, by which both parties officially recognized each other. The Oslo agreement established the framework for a Palestinian-administered territory in the West Bank and Gaza Strip areas—which Israel had occupied since the 1967 Six-Day War—with an eye toward full independence in the future. In 2000, however, the peace process stalled after the failure of the Camp David Summit hosted by President Bill Clinton. Palestinian terrorists began attacking Israelis, and Israel responded with harsh crackdowns on Palestinians. Over the next few years the bloodletting escalated enormously, with a string of Palestinian suicide bombings that killed scores of civilians and Israeli responses that included assassinations and military occupations of Palestinian towns. Amid pro-Palestinian demonstrations in the streets of Cairo, the Egyptian government condemned the actions of Israel.

This was not the only conflict testing Egypt's ability to remain both a leader in the Arab world and an ally of the United States. On September 11, 2001, terrorists sponsored by the **Islamist** group al-Qaeda flew hijacked jetliners into the World Trade Center in New York City and the Pentagon in Washington, D.C. President Hosni Mubarak officially condemned the acts of terrorism, but that position was by no means universally shared in his country. Many Egyptians said publicly that the attacks were just punishment for U.S. support of

In June 2009, U.S. President Barack Obama delivered a historic speech at Cairo University, in which he called for a "new beginning between the United States and Muslims," declaring that "this cycle of suspicion and discord must end." The speech was generally praised by people in the Arab world.

Israel and Arab dictatorship; the mainstream Egyptian media, which operates under government supervision, even claimed that the World Trade Center attack was the work of a Jewish conspiracy.

Egypt itself has long confronted an Islamist movement of its own. Islamic terrorism has occurred throughout Egypt since the 1990s. Groups like the Egyptian Islamic Jihad and Al-Gama'a al-Islamiyya (the Islamic Group), have worked with al-Qaeda.

When the United States responded to the September 11 terrorism by attacking Afghanistan, a nation that was harboring al-Qaeda, Egypt publicly voiced support. But it did not offer to contribute Egyptian troops to the effort.

Egypt voiced disapproval when the United States, under President George W. Bush, invaded Iraq in 2003 and overthrew its dictator, Saddam Hussein. President Mubarak even predicted that the war would cause more terrorism than it would prevent. Egypt and the United States have also disagreed on many of Israel's military decisions, including attacks against the Palestinian group Hamas in the Gaza Strip during 2006 and 2014.

During the 2011 revolution, U.S. government officials urged Hosni Mubarak to reform his government, and threatened to withhold U.S. financial aid if the regime used violence against protesters.

Since Mubarak left office, the U.S.-Egypt relationship has grown more tenuous, as each country seems to be in "wait and see" mode with regard to the other. On September 11, 2012, an Egyptian mob attacked the U.S. Embassy in Cairo, lowering the U.S. flag. The Morsi administration also had considerably cooler relations toward Israel than Mubarak's government had, although Morsi did help to negotiate a cease-fire between Hamas and Israel after a 2012 incident.

Although the U.S. did not approve of Morsi's policies, the Obama administration strongly protested the 2013 military coup that removed him from power. (Israel, on the other hand, encouraged international support for the Egyptian military, a sign of its mistrust of Morsi and the Muslim Brotherhood, which is committed to the destruction of the Jewish state.) To protest the coup, the U.S. withheld aid and canceled the sale of military hardware to the Egyptian Army. However, by 2014 the U.S. had quetly resumed its aid program, and the relationship seems to be warming again.

The United States and Egypt have much at stake in their close relationship and are likely to try to maintain it despite periodic strains. For Egypt, the United States is a source of much-needed economic aid. For the United States, Egypt provides stability and a moderate influence among the Arab nations of the strategically vital Middle East.

Text-Dependent Questions

1. What is the PLO?
2. Which U.S. president helped negotiate a treaty between Egypt and Israel in 1978?

Research Project

Use the Internet or your school library to research the life of Anwar el-Sadat. Based on what you learn, write two paragraphs discussing why you think Sadat was willing to risk the anger of other Arab League members to broker a treaty with Israel.

ca. 3100 BCE: Lower and Upper Egypt are united into a single kingdom with its capital at Memphis.

2700–2200 BCE: Old Kingdom of ancient Egypt; Egypt's rulers build the great pyramids.

2040–1640 BCE: Middle Kingdom of ancient Egypt.

1560–1070 BCE: New Kingdom of ancient Egypt; the Egyptian kings begin to call themselves pharaohs.

332 BCE: Alexander the Great of Macedon conquers Egypt.

30 BCE: Egypt becomes a province of Rome.

639–641 CE: Arab Muslim armies conquer Egypt.

969: The Muslim Fatimid dynasty takes over Egypt; the Fatimids make Al-Qahirah, or Cairo, their capital city.

1250: The Mamluks take over Egypt.

1798: Napoléon Bonaparte occupies Alexandria and establishes a French presence in Egypt.

1801: British and Ottoman armies force the French to withdraw from Egypt.

1805: Muhammad Ali, one of the Ottoman Turks who fought against the French, becomes the ruler of Egypt.

1811: Muhammad Ali kills Mamluk rivals to consolidate his rule; begins program to modernize Egypt.

1869: The Suez Canal is completed.

1875: Britain becomes the main shareholder in the Suez Canal.

1882: British warships bombard Alexandria; the British soon take Cairo and begin their occupation of Egypt.

1888: Britain and other nations sign the Constantinople Convention, pledging to keep the Suez Canal open under all circumstances.

1914: After the outbreak of World War I, Britain declares Egypt a protectorate.

1922: Britain officially recognizes Egypt's independence but continues to exert some control; King Fuad I becomes Egypt's ruler.

1936: Egypt and Britain sign the Anglo-Egyptian Treaty, which permits 10,000 British troops to be garrisoned along the Suez Canal.

1937: Egypt joins the League of Nations.

1939: World War II begins; during the war, the British use Egypt for military operations.

CHRONOLOGY

1942: The British defeat German forces in a major tank battle at El Alamein.

1945: Egypt and other Arab nations form the Arab League; Egypt also becomes a founding member of the United Nations.

1948: The UN creates the State of Israel; Egypt and other Arab nations go to war against the new state and are defeated, though Egypt takes control of the Gaza Strip.

1952: Led by Gamal Abdel Nasser, the Free Officers overthrow King Farouk.

1953: Egypt becomes an independent republic.

1956: Nasser becomes the president of Egypt, nationalizes the Suez Canal; Britain, France, and Israel respond by mounting an attack on the Sinai Peninsula.

1967: Nasser asks for the removal of UN troops on the Egyptian-Israeli border, announces the closing of the Gulf of Aqaba to Israeli ships. Israel triggers the Six-Day War with preemptive attacks on Egypt, Jordan, and Syria, decisively defeating its Arab enemies. As a result of the war the Suez Canal is closed because of sunken ships, and Egypt loses Gaza.

1970: Anwar el-Sadat becomes Egypt's president after the death of Nasser.

1973: Egypt, along with Syria, fights the October (Yom Kippur) War against Israel.

1975: The Suez Canal reopens.

1977: Sadat addresses the Israeli Knesset, declares his desire for peace between Egypt and Israel.

1978: Meeting at the U.S. presidential retreat of Camp David, Sadat and Israeli prime minister Menachem Begin, with mediation from President Jimmy Carter, agree to a peace treaty, which comes to be known as the Camp David Accords.

1979: Egypt and Israel sign the Camp David Accords; the Arab League responds by expelling Egypt.

1981: Sadat is assassinated by Islamic fundamentalists; Hosni Mubarak becomes Egypt's new president.

1982: Israeli forces withdraw from the Sinai Peninsula.

1989: Egypt is readmitted to the Arab League.

1991: During the Gulf War, Egypt joins a U.S.-led coalition that drives Iraq out of Kuwait.

1992: Egyptian statesman and diplomat Boutros Boutros-Ghali becomes the first Arab and the first African to hold the post of secretary-general of the United Nations.

1997: Terrorists kill 58 foreign tourists at Luxor.

2001: Al-Qaeda terrorists strike the United States on September 11; President Mubarak condemns the attacks, supports U.S. invasion of Afghanistan, but Egyptian popular opinion is divided.

2002: Increased violence between Palestinians and Israelis threatens to destabilize Middle East; many Egyptians stage demonstrations to protest Israeli punitive incursions into Palestinian cities.

2004: 34 people are killed in a series of three bombings in the Sinai Peninsula, apparently targeting Israeli tourists.

2005: Attacks on a popular Red Sea tourist resort kill 88; a voter referendum paves the way for multi-party elections; Hosni Mubarak is reelected for a fifth term as president of Egypt.

2006: The Egyptian government criticizes Israel's conduct in a 34-day war with Lebanon.

2007: After a low-turnout voter referendum, Egypt's constitution is controversially amended to ban religiously based political parties and to give the president more power. The National Democratic Party wins the most votes in parliamentary elections.

2008: More than 800 members of the banned Muslim Brotherhood party are arrested; bandits kidnap 10 tourists and 8 guides in the Sahara, but release them after 10 days under pressure from Egyptian troops.

2011: After 18 days of widespread protest, President Hosni Mubarak steps down and transfers power to the military.

2012: Mohamed Morsi, a member of the Muslim Brotherhood, is sworn in as president after he wins Egypt's first competitive presidential election.

2013: Following widespread protests in June, Morsi is ousted in a military coup.

2014: General Abdel-Fattah el-Sisi, Egypt's former defense minister, is elected president in May.

2015: Parliamentary elections are scheduled.

SERIES GLOSSARY

autonomy—the right of self-government.

BCE and CE—an alternative to the traditional Western designation of calendar eras, which used the birth of Jesus as a dividing line. BCE stands for "Before the Common Era," and is equivalent to BC ("Before Christ"). Dates labeled CE, or "Common Era," are equivalent to Anno Domini (AD, or "the Year of Our Lord").

caliphate—an Islamic theocratic state, in which the ruler, or caliph, has authority over both the spiritual and temporal lives of his subjects and all people must obey Islamic laws.

civil society—the sum total of institutions, organizations, and groups promoting social and civic causes in a country (for example, human rights groups, labor unions, arts foundations) that are not funded or controlled by the government or business interests.

colonialism—control or domination by one country over an area or people outside its boundaries; the policy of colonizing foreign lands.

ideology—a system of beliefs, values, and ideas forming the basis of a social, economic, or political philosophy.

Islamist—a Muslim who advocates the reformation of society and government in accordance with Islamic laws and principles.

jihadism—adherence to the idea that Muslims should carry out a war against un-Islamic groups and ideas, especially Westerners and Western liberal culture.

nationalism—the belief that shared ethnicity, language, and history should form the basis for political organization; the desire of people with a common culture to have their own state.

Pan-Arabism—a movement seeking to unite all Arab peoples into a single state.

self-determination—determination by a people of their own future political status.

Sharia—Islamic law, based on the Qur'an and other Islamic writings and traditions. The Sharia sets forth the moral goals of an Islamic society, and governs a Muslim's religious political, social, and private life.

Shia—the smaller of Islam's two major branches, whose rift with the larger Sunni branch originated in seventh-century disputes over who should succeed the prophet Muhammad as leader of the Muslim community.

Sunni—a Muslim who belongs to the largest branch of Islam.

Wahhabism—a highly conservative form of Sunni Islam practiced in Saudi Arabia.

Zionism—the movement to establish a Jewish state in Palestine; support for the State of Israel.

FURTHER READING

Boutros-Ghali, Boutros. *Egypt's Road to Jerusalem.* New York: Random House, 1997.

Danahar, Paul. *The New Middle East: The World After the Arab Spring.* New York: Bloomsbury Press, 2013.

Goldschmidt, Arthur, Jr. *Modern Egypt: The Formation of a Nation-State.* 2nd edition. Boulder, Colo.: Westview Press, 2004.

Joffe, George. *A Century of Arab Revolution: The Legacy of Empires.* London: I.B. Tauris, 2015.

Lynch, Marc. *The Arab Uprising: The Unfinished Revolutions of the New Middle East.* New York: PublicAffairs, 2013.

Mansfield, Peter. *A History of the Middle East.* 4th ed. revised and updated by Nicholas Pelham. New York: Penguin Books, 2013.

Osman, Tarek. *Egypt on the Brink: From Nasser to the Muslim Brotherhood.* New Haven: Yale University Press, 2013.

Rodenbeck, Max. *Cairo: The City Victorious.* London: Picador, 1998.

Sattin, Anthony. *Egypt.* Oakland, Calif.: Lonely Planet Publications, 2015.

Weiss, Thomas G., et al. *The United Nations and Changing World Politics.* Boulder, Colo.: Westview Press, 2007.

Wien, Peter. *Arab Nationalism: The Politics of History and Culture in the Modern Middle East.* New York: Routledge, 2015.

Zayan, Jailan. *Egypt: A Quick Guide to Customs & Etiquette.* London: Kuperard, 2007.

http://www.state.gov/r/pa/ei/bgn/5309.htm

The U.S. State Department website has a thorough section on the background of Egypt, including its economics, politics, and other information.

https://www.cia.gov/library/publications/the-world-factbook/geos/eg.html

The CIA World Factbook website provides a great deal of statistical information about Egypt and its people. It is regularly updated.

www.mideasti.org

An extensive resource geared to educate Americans about the Middle East. This academic site includes loads of information for research.

www.un.org/english

The English-language web page for the United Nations can be searched for Egypt-related stories and information.

www.bbc.com/news

The official website of BBC News provides articles and videos on important international news and events related to the Middle East and elsewhere.

www.aljazeera.com

The English-language website of the Arabic news service Al Jazeera provides articles and videos on breaking news, as well as feature stories that provide background material, including profiles of leaders and essays reacting to major events.

www.fpri.org

The website of the Foreign Policy Research Institute includes informative essays by FPRI scholars on events in the Middle East.

Publisher's Note: The websites listed on this page were active at the time of publication. The publisher is not responsible for websites that have changed their address or discontinued operation since the date of publication. The publisher reviews and updates the websites each time the book is reprinted.

INDEX

Numbers in **bold italic** refer to captions.

INDEX

PICTURE CREDITS

Senior Consultant Camille Pecastaing, Ph.D., is acting director of the Middle East Studies Program at the Paul H. Nitze School of Advanced International Studies at Johns Hopkins University. A student of behavioral sciences and historical sociology, Dr. Pecastaing's research focuses on the cognitive and emotive foundations of xenophobic political cultures and ethnoreligious violence, using the Muslim world and its European and Asian peripheries as a case study. He has written on political Islam, Islamist terrorism, social change, and globalization. Pecastaing's essays have appeared in many journals, including *World Affairs* and *Policy Review*. He is the author of *Jihad in the Arabian Sea* (Hoover Institution Press, 2011).

The Foreign Policy Research Institute (FPRI) provided editorial guidance for this series. FPRI is one of the nation's oldest "think tanks." The Institute's Middle East Program focuses on Gulf security, monitors the Arab-Israeli peace process, and sponsors an annual conference for teachers on the Middle East, plus periodic briefings on key developments in the region.

Among FPRI's trustees are a former Undersecretary of Defense, a former Secretary of the Navy, a former Assistant Secretary of State, a foundation president, and numerous active or retired corporate CEOs, lawyers, and civic leaders. Scholars affiliated with FPRI include a Pulitzer Prize–winning historian; a former president of Swarthmore College; a Bancroft Prize–winning historian; and a former Ambassador and senior staff member of the National Security Council. And FPRI counts among its extended network of scholars—especially its Inter-University Study Groups—representatives of many diverse disciplines, including political science, history, economics, law, management, religion, sociology, and psychology.

CLARISSA AYKROYD is a graduate of the University of Victoria in British Columbia, Canada. She has written and published fiction, reviews and criticism, travel writing, and educational writing for software programs. Her previous nonfiction works for children include books on the exploration of California, Native American horsemanship, and the history of Mexican government. Her interests include history, travel, music, Arthurian legend, and Sherlock Holmes.